Cover illustration by Sybil Anderson
Cover photographs by Tom Hustler and Jane Wilson
Models: Sarah and Helen Gallagher
Edited by Ann Moynihan and Vronwyn M Thompson
Designed by Brian Folkard Design

Published in Great Britain by World International Publishing Limited, An Egmont Company, Egmont House, PO Box 111, Great Ducie Street, Manchester M60 3BL

ISBN 07498 0906 X

Printed in Italy

£4.50 UK ONLY

OWL FILE

BY THE EDITOR

illustrated by Jane Bennett

Almost since Brownies began, we've named our Guiders after owls – Brown Owl, Tawny Owl, Snowy, Barny and Eagle! Let's look at the real owls that lend many of our Guiders their names!

Owls are birds of prey which hunt mainly by night, although sometimes you'll see an owl resting in a tree during the day. You can sometimes see owls hunting at night if you're out in a car, as they fly through the light from the headlights.

Owls have flat faces, with both eyes pointing forwards, and short hooked beaks, which makes them look different from other birds. When resting they perch almost upright, with their short tails pointing downwards. Some owls have high ear 'tufts', but these aren't real ears.

BARN OWL

Latin name: Tyto alba.
Colour: Golden-brown above, white chest and heart-shaped face. If you suddenly catch sight of one in the car headlights it can look all-white. Often seen at dusk.
Call: Not so much a call, more a long blood-curdling screech – that's why it's sometimes called a Screech Owl.
Nest: In barns, church towers, old buildings.
Food: Mice, voles, other small animals.
Size: 34-36cm tall.
Can be found: All over Britain and Ireland except for the very north of Scotland.

TAWNY OWL

Latin name: Strix aluco.
Colour: Can be brown or grey, with black eyes.
Call: 'Ke-wick' (can sound like 'tu-whit, tu-whoo'). Young Tawny Owls sometimes sound like a squeaky gate!
Nest: In holes in trees. Hunts by night and rests in trees by day. Sometimes, if you see a lot of small birds making a fuss around a tree you'll find a Tawny Owl trying to get some rest!
Food: Small birds, mice, voles.
Size: About 38cm tall.
Can be found: In woods and fields, parks and gardens all over England, Scotland and Wales.

SNOWY OWL

Latin name: Nyctea scandiaca.
Colour: Mostly white. Females have blackish bars on wings and underneath.
Call: Females bark, males hoot.
Food: Small animals like lemmings, birds such as oystercatcher and ptarmigan. Hunts by day, and white plumage is camouflage against snow.
Size: 53-66cm tall.
Can be found: North Norway, Lapland, Iceland. Sometimes in north of Scotland, Orkney and Shetland Islands.

LITTLE OWL

Latin name: Athene noctua.
Colour: Brown, with lighter face and bars on wings.
Call: 'Kiew, kiew' – often heard during the day as well as at night.
Nest: Holes in trees, old buildings. Sometimes perches on a post or branch to look around; waggles head and bobs up and down.
Food: Insects and small animals. Sometimes you can see a Little Owl hovering in the twilight to catch insects.
Size: 22cm tall.
Can be found: In England and Wales.

LONG-EARED OWL

Latin name: Asio otus.
Colour: Brown, with long ear-tufts and orange-yellow eyes. Longer face and wings than Tawny Owl.
Call: Long, moaning hoot, like 'hoooo-hoooo...'
Nest: Usually uses old nest of another bird. During the day it sleeps in woods, especially fir trees. In winter, groups of Long-eared Owls will sleep in the same tree.
Food: Small animals and birds.
Size: 36cm tall.
Can be found: Almost all over Great Britain and Ireland.

SHORT-EARED OWL

Latin name: Asio flammeus.
Colour: Brown, with short ear-tufts which you don't usually see when it's flying.
Flight: Soars and glides on long wings, also flapping 'owl' flight.
Call: Barks and hoots, sounding like 'hoo-hoo-hoo'.
Nest: Holes in trees, old buildings.
Food: Hunts for small mammals and birds over marshes, moors and open ground during the day and in the evening.
Size: 38cm tall.
Can be found: In Great Britain and south and east Ireland.

EAGLE OWL

Latin name: Bubo bubo.
Colour: Brown, with large ear-tufts and large orange eyes.
Call: Deep 'oo-uh', and a 'kveck, kveck'.
Food: Hunts at dawn and dusk, for animals as large as roe deer, hare, rabbit and birds like capercaillie.
Size: 66-71cm tall – the largest European owl.
Can be found: In Norway and parts of Sweden, and is quite rare.

5

There are many other owls – and although there isn't a bird actually called a Brown Owl (except the one in the Brownie Story!) there's a Brown Fish Owl from the eastern Mediterranean Sea, an African Marsh Owl, Scops Owl, Hawk Owl, Pygmy Owl and Tengmalm's Owl, none of which are native to the UK.

OWL FACTS

- Owls can be found in every continent except Antarctica.
- Owls' ears are very sensitive – they can pinpoint a tiny animal and catch it just by listening.
- An owl swallows its prey whole, and coughs up 'pellets' of the bits it can't digest, such as fur, bones and beaks. If you find any owl pellets you can carefully break them apart to see what the owl has eaten.
- Barn Owls are sometimes called 'Jenny Owls'.
- Owls can swivel their heads round so that they can see in almost any direction.

In the UK, Barn Owls are becoming rarer. In 1932 there were more than 12,000 breeding pairs of Barn Owls – now there are only about 4,000. This is because many of their habitats are being destroyed – old barns are being knocked down or turned into houses – and many owls are killed by cars or lorries when they fly low across the countryside to hunt for food.

So, a few years ago, the Hawk and Owl Trust started the Barn Owl Conservation Network campaign to provide places for Barn Owls to live. The volunteers who support the Trust are putting up nest boxes to replace the old barns, buildings and trees which the owls used to live in. The nest boxes are going up in special places to encourage Barn Owls to settle and breed, so that there will be more of them to breed next year, and so on. There are colonies of Barn Owls throughout the country, but they are often a long way from each other, so the Trust is trying to link them with special 'habitat corridors'. This will mean that the owls can fly and hunt further afield, which gives them more chance to meet a partner and breed baby owls.

However, owl habitats are always under threat, so the Trust is working with landowners and farmers to conserve old habitats and replace lost ones with new nest boxes. Hundreds of owls are already using the boxes to raise their families – which is good for Barn Owls and good for us. As naturalist Gerald Durrell says:

'For centuries the Barn Owl has lived in close proximity to man and it is only reasonable that we should treat such close neighbours as good friends. As human beings we create many things which could be created again, but if we destroy a thing like the Barn Owl we could not recreate it with all the technology we have developed. Therefore this sort of conservation is the most important of all.'

The Hawk and Owl Trust works for the conservation of all birds of prey, including owls, and to help people find out more about these beautiful creatures they have opened the National Centre for Owl Conservation in Norfolk. Here there is an exhibition about the conservation of birds of prey, especially Barn Owls, and a 'Pellet Corner' where you can cut up and examine owl pellets to see what the owls have been eating. There are wild owls on the estate where the Centre is, and a special 'Raptor Ramble' nature trail which goes by plenty of nest boxes, so that visitors can see the owls in their natural environment.

The National Centre for Owl Conservation is two miles north of Aylsham in Norfolk, between Norwich and Cromer. It is open from April to the end of October.

Just for fun, here are some puzzles about Brownie Six emblems. Try to do them without looking at your Handbook. You will find the answers on page 61.

puzzle time

by Gill Pawley   illustrated by Helen Herbert

JUMBLED UP SIXES

Work out which Six names are jumbled up here.

SPIM _____

LESEIPK _____

VEELS _____

TIRESSP _____

MOGENS _____

SIXEPI _____

WHAT'S MISSING?

Take a careful look at these Brownies below. What's missing?

THE LOST LEPRECHAUN

Can you help this Leprechaun to find his way out of the maze to the Brownie pool?

There are more Six puzzles on page 55.

Rained out!

by Heather Welford illustrated by Sybil Anderson

'Oh, no. Not again!' Brown Owl groaned as she looked up at the ceiling of the church hall. Drip, drip, drip. Splosh. Splosh. The rain was coming through, as it had done on at least four occasions in the past eight or nine meetings.

'Come on, Brownies, you know what to do by now!'

The circle of eighteen girls stopped playing Chinese Whispers, and got up, sighing.

'Brown Owl, do we have to?' said Kirstie Taverner, who never minded saying what the others were all thinking.

'Yes, I'm afraid so, Kirstie. Not everyone feels like you,' said Brown Owl over her shoulder, as she opened the caretaker's cupboard and started handing out buckets and bowls to the rest of the Brownies. 'Some people are a tiny bit more helpful.' She reached inside for the mop. 'I expect we'll be needing this, as well,' she said to Tawny Owl.

One or two of the younger Brownies saw the fun in the exercise. Twins Mandy and Suzanne really enjoyed spotting yet another leak, putting a bucket in exactly the right place, and then rushing around the edges of the hall to find another one. And this evening's rain was heavy enough to make them work hard. The noise of the storm raged outside, and rattled the high windows.

'I think the storm's loosened a few more tiles,' said Tawny Owl. 'There are definitely more holes this time...ooh!' She looked up, and a particularly large drop of rain fell right in her eye.

'This is too much!' she said to Brown Owl, wiping her face. 'I know the Mothers' Union have been complaining about the roof as well. Their cake competition last week was a bit of a wash-out.'

'I heard,' said Brown Owl. 'Apparently most of the entries were spread out in the kitchen ready for judging, and when the rain came no one remembered to check in there until it was too late.'

'Excuse me, Brown Owl,' said Kirstie, who'd come up to the two leaders.

'Yes, Kirstie, what is it? If you've finished with that mop wring it out and put it away – it's dripping all over my shoes at the moment...'

'Sorry, Brown Owl. I'm just on my way to the cupboard...but I just wanted to say that we're really, really, really sick of wet meetings!'

And with that she turned away and stalked off.

Tawny Owl and Brown Owl exchanged the sort of glances that meant 'little madam!'.

After the meeting had ended and most of the girls had gone, Tawny brought up the subject of the roof again.

'Brenda, we have to do something. It's impossible to have meetings here.'

Brown Owl nodded her agreement. 'I know. It's being dealt with – and it's a big job, too. It's not just the roof they're going to renew, either. It's the outside walls, the central heating, the electrics, the loos, and the kitchen...'

'...And the draughty window frames,' interrupted Tawny.

'Quite right. The vicar says he's expecting work to begin in a month or so. It'll take about six weeks.'

'Well, I suppose that's progress. But we can't go on using it in this state, surely?'

'No. We won't be able to use the hall, nobody will, while it's being repaired and decorated. But I had thought we might manage a couple more weeks or so until the work got under way. Tonight was the last straw, though. We'll have to suspend Brownies for at least two to three months from next week onwards.'

The following week, the Brownies' faces fell when Brown Owl told them that tonight would be their last meeting for at least another ten weeks.

Mandy and Suzanne looked at each other sadly. 'But we like Brownies,' said Mandy.

'And we don't mind the rain,' said Suzanne.

'That's very spirited of you both,' Brown Owl smiled at them, kindly. 'But we can't have decent meetings when we're mopping up and dodging the rain all the time.'

Kirstie was working out a sum on her fingers.

'Ten weeks. That means not until after Christmas, doesn't it?'

Brown Owl agreed that yes, it did mean that.

'So what about the Christmas carol concert and entertainment for the mums and dads?'

Brown Owl admitted that, unfortunately, this year's concert would have to go. Kirstie's face fell. She had a good voice, and there was nothing she liked better than performing. Last year's rehearsals, and the concert itself, had been a highlight of her Christmas.

Brown Owl went on. 'Think of it, girls. Your mums and dads and grans and grandads...singing *Hark the Herald Angels Sing* with huge drops of rain running down their noses! It wouldn't work, would it?' The Brownies had to agree. It wouldn't work.

Kirstie walked home that night with her dad, thinking carefully.

'You're quiet tonight,' said her father, used to a string of non-stop chatter about the events and happenings at the meeting. Kirstie had told him there'd be no more meetings for a while, and then had remained quiet.

'Mm. I'm just wondering about something. Something important.'

'Go on, then, tell your old dad.'

'Well, you know the Cedars?'

Dad smiled. 'Should do. I only work there 40 hours or more a week.' Kirstie's father was chef at the old people's home, and Kirstie often visited him, and the residents, when she was on holiday from school.

'You know it's got that great big day room, the one that looks out on to the garden?'

'Yes...what about it?'

'Could we, um, sort of borrow it, do you think?'

Her dad was puzzled. 'Not sure what you mean.'

Kirstie coughed, nervously.

'For about three months, one evening a week, for an hour and a half...just while the hall's out of action. Go on, Dad, it'd be great – will you ask Mrs Harrison? We wouldn't be too noisy – anyway the day room's well away from anywhere else where people might be resting or watching TV or anything.'

Mrs Harrison, the manager of the Cedars, was an approachable sort of person and Mr Taverner got on well with her. He paused before answering. Kirstie might just have a possible idea there.

'Look, I'll ask her – but I can't promise anything. But I will ask.'

The next week saw a series of phone calls between Brown Owl and Mrs Harrison, and each Brownie received a letter telling her of the new temporary meeting place.

Mandy and Suzanne were thrilled to bits – especially as their much-loved great-grandmother lived at the Cedars.

Meetings went surprisingly well. 'Kirstie, you're a genius!' said Brown Owl, on the fourth week. 'We've been made very welcome indeed...and I think we should thank Mrs Harrison, and everyone here.'

'I know how!' said Kirstie, 'if it's not too late...'

'Go on, then, tell me!'

'We could have the concert after all, here in the day room – there's a piano, and space at the top end, but we could do it specially for the residents.'

Brown Owl looked pleased and thoughtful. 'I think that's a super idea, Kirstie. Let's see what the others think.'

'Do you think they'll want to do it?' Kirstie fervently hoped so.

'We'll ask them now...but what are you looking at?' Brown Owl watched as Kirstie turned her head ceiling-wards.

'Just checking for holes!' she replied. 'We don't want any drips in *Hark the Herald*!'

GOD SAVE THE QUEEN

by Gillian Ellis   illustrated by Anna King

You're all so used to being subjects of Her Majesty the Queen, it probably hasn't occurred to you that a Queen on the throne of Great Britain is fairly unusual. But had you realised that Queen Elizabeth II is only the sixth crowned female ruler of the United Kingdom and that you probably won't see another in your lifetime?

In the early days, our islands were split into many small areas, often known as Kingdoms. In the year 938, England became united under one ruler and later joined with Wales in 1307 under the rule of Edward II. The United Kingdom was formed in 1603 when James VI of Scotland inherited the English crown, then Northern Ireland became a member of the UK in 1801.

In our country, sons of monarchs always take precedence or come before older sisters, so it doesn't often happen that a girl becomes a ruler in her own right. This can only occur if a British King has no sons at all. Our present Queen had no brothers so she came to the throne.

Our only other crowned Queens have been Mary I, Elizabeth I, Anne, Mary II and Victoria, although two others, Matilda in 1141 and Lady Jane Grey in 1553, ascended the throne briefly but were never crowned.

Mary I and Elizabeth I were half-sisters who ruled during the 16th century and, oddly enough, the next two Queens were sisters, too.

Mary II ruled jointly with her husband William III, by her own wish and, as they had no children, Mary's sister Anne became Queen after them. Poor Queen Anne had 14 babies, of whom only five were born alive and even those died in childhood.

Over a century later, the next Queen, Victoria, had nine children, five daughters and four sons. Queen Victoria came to the throne in 1837 when she was 18, and ruled for 63 years. We almost had a Queen Georgina Alexandrina instead, but at the christening, her Uncle George, the Prince Regent, suddenly decided she was to be called Victoria after her mother! Her eldest child was a daughter, called HRH Princess Victoria Adelaide Mary Louisa, so it was the next child, HRH Prince Albert Edward, who became King Edward VII (the seventh) in 1901. He was the great-grandfather of our present Queen.

Victoria came to be known as 'The Grandmother of Europe' because her children married into every royal family in Europe! Both Queen Elizabeth II and her husband Prince Philip are great-great-grandchildren of Queen Victoria.

The Scots have had a couple more Queens than the English; they had Queen Margaret and Queen Mary before the United Kingdom was formed. Margaret was only Queen of Scots for a short time and hardly saw Scotland at all. She was the daughter of a King of Norway and died in 1290, four years after becoming Queen.

Mary, Queen of Scots, was one of the most famous Queens of all time. Amongst other things, she was said to have ordered the murder of her husband, then married his murderer, but there are many different stories about this. Because she was related to the English royal family, she was a rival of Queen Elizabeth of England, who eventually had her beheaded.

So next time you sing *God Save the Queen*, remember that you're among a special few in the United Kingdom's history who can ever sing those words. When your grandparents were your age (and when you have grandchildren, if you can imagine that!) the words were (or will be) just a little different, though the sentiments remain the same.

LEND A HAND

CROSSWORD

Get yourself into a helpful mood to do this crossword! Most of the clues are linked with ways you can lend a hand.

by Heather Welford
illustrated by Helen Herbert

CLUES

Across

4 If you rub a table with 6 across, it will do this (5)

6 Used with a cloth on wooden furniture and floors (6)

7 Brownies do one of these each day (4,4)

9 Tin mop art (anagram) means 'essential' (9)

10 You might say this if you don't like something! (3)

Down

1 It's helpful to do this after a meal (7,2)

2 If you're good to the people next door, you're being this (11)

3 If something's dirty, then ——— it (5)

5 See 8

8 and 5 Don't forget to say this if someone lends you a hand! (5,3)

Answers on page 61.

BEAN *FEAST!*

by Gill Pawley   illustrated by Anna King

How about trying some Wild West fun, like Helen on page 39? On these two pages there are some 'cowboy' activities to try. There are things to do and things to make. You might like to try some of them with your Six, or some friends, or even your brother or sister!

COWBOYS OF OLD

If you have ever watched an old Wild West film, then you'll have some ideas about cowboys. But did you know that in days of old there were female 'cowboys' as well as male?

It was a hard life for a cowboy – his or her job was to look after hundreds of cattle that grazed on the open lands of America. From time to time the cattle needed to be rounded up and taken to market or new feeding grounds along the long dusty cattle trails which led from place to place.

Nowadays, there are not many real cowboys but in places like Texas, in the United States of America, some people still wear the traditional ten-gallon hats that the cowboys wore on the cattle trails.

UNDER THE STARS

When the cowboys were out on the trail, they had to sleep under the stars in the open. Every night, they would set up a camp. Their first job was to make sure that the cattle had water to drink, settle them down and make them safe for the night. The cowboys looked after the cattle carefully because they were worth a lot of money and the cowboys would only get paid if they delivered the cattle safely. The cowboys would then look after their horses, feeding and watering them and sometimes tethering them so that they couldn't wander away.

Next, someone would build a fire. The fire was useful for three reasons – to cook the evening meal, to keep the cowboys warm at night and to keep wild animals away. They would cook their evening meal – something warm and filling like beans and meatballs, then wrap themselves in their blankets and sleep around the fire. One cowboy would stay awake to keep watch.

PITCH YOUR OWN CAMP

If you would like to have a go at being a cowboy, the first thing to do is make your own camp!

Ask Mum or Dad if you can make a tent in your garden or in your bedroom. If you have your own tent, you can put that up. If not, ask if you can borrow a large blanket and some chairs – a clothes horse shaped like a gate is very useful for making a blanket tent!

14

Unless you have a big garden and someone older to help you, it's probably best to have a pretend fire, not a real one. Make a pretend fire with sticks of wood and red tissue or crepe paper. Don't try to light it – fire is very dangerous!

WILD WEST GRUB

Hungry cowboys need plenty of food to keep them going on the trail and one of the traditional meals was pork 'n' beans. Have a go at our version (ask Mum or Dad first):

You will need:
a *small tin of pork luncheon meat*
a *tin of baked beans with pork sausages*
cooking oil

Ask an adult to help you. This amount will feed you and three friends.

Here is what you do:

1 Cut the pork luncheon meat into small cubes.

2 Put the tin of beans and sausages into a small pan and gently warm them through until they are really hot.

3 Next, heat the cooking oil in a frying pan and when it is hot add the luncheon meat and fry until it is brown all over. Then drain well on kitchen paper.

4 Finally, add the luncheon meat to the beans and sausages.

5 Serve the cowboy grub up to your friends with some bread.

MORE COWBOY FARE

Other favourite cowboy food is Mexican chilli (spiced meat and kidney beans) and tacos (crispy pancakes filled with mince). Cowboys also like barbecue beef. Perhaps Mum or Dad could help you try these dishes as well.

YEE-HAW PARTNER

Traditional cowboys had nicknames like Cactus Pete, Slim Jim and Texas Bill. Make up some nicknames for your cowboy gang, based on some of your hobbies.

LASSO AWAY

One of the arts that a cowboy needed to perfect was lassoing cattle. This involves making a loop at the end of a long piece of rope.

If they needed to, cowboys could throw the rope in such a way that the loop would land over a runaway cow's head and the cow would be caught before it got a chance to get away.

Try to make a lasso like this:

Have a go at lassoing things like your bike, or a chair. It really is quite hard! **Never try to throw it over someone's head or neck.**

illustrated by Kate Simpson

The Lord is good to me
And so I thank the Lord
For giving me the things I need –
The sun, the rain and the appleseed
The Lord is good to me.

And every seed that grows
Will grow into a tree
So one day soon, there'll be apples there
For everyone in the world to share
The Lord is good to me.

Johnny Appleseed

Lots of you will know this as a grace sung before meals at Pack Holiday. But how many of you know that it is about a real person?

John Chapman was born in America some time around 1780. When he was a young man, he left the big towns of the eastern coast of America and travelled west.

On his travels, he planted tiny apple seeds, to grow and give food for people, shade for animals and protection for other plants. He got his first seeds from apples which had been used to make cider, but collected others and planted them as he travelled around.

People began to call him 'Johnny Appleseed', and said that he also planted herbs which could be used as medicine in a land where doctors were few and far between.

Like St Francis, he cared for animals and he was an expert plant doctor, too. Farmers were glad when they saw him coming, because he would help them if they were having trouble with crops or other plants on their farms.

Today we would say that Johnny Appleseed was an ecologist, looking after nature and living in harmony with plants, people and animals.

When you made your Brownie Promise, you became a member of a world-wide family of girls and women who all have something in common – they're Brownies, Guides or Girl Scouts. There are something like 14,000,000 of them in countries from Greenland to Australia, from Japan to Chile. (How many Good Turns is that a year?!)

You may not meet every Brownie, Guide or Girl Scout, but you might be able, one day, to meet some of them at one of our World Centres – special Guide homes for Girl Guides and Girl Scouts in Switzerland, Mexico, England and India. They are owned by the World Association of Girl Guides and Girl Scouts (WAGGGS).

HOMES AROUND THE WORLD

by the Editor
photographs by Sandy Everitt, Elizabeth Aveston, Hettie Smith and the Editor

OUR CHALET, SWITZERLAND

'High up, high on the mountain
We've founded Our Chalet.'

Our Chalet is 1,300 metres above sea level in a village called Adelboden in Switzerland. It was opened in 1932 and was the first of our Guide houses. It is a real Swiss chalet, with a long sloping roof and windowboxes. Over the door is written in German 'Gott Behute dieses Hus and All da gehen yn und us', which means 'God bless this house and all who go in and out'.

Sixty people can stay at Our Chalet and there is room for more in the Squirrel House and the Baby Chalet. There is a small house called Stockli, where the Chalet staff live.

The Guides and Girl Scouts who visit Our Chalet can go walking and climbing in the beautiful mountains in summer or skiing and sledging in winter.

OUR CABAÑA, MEXICO

'Neath the grand Sierra Madre on the plains of Mexico
Lies our beautiful Cabaña where the Guides and Girl Scouts go'

Our Cabaña was opened in 1957 by the World Chief Guide, Olave, Lady Baden-Powell. It overlooks the city of Cuernavaca and looks towards the snow-capped mountains of Mexico.

Everyone who stays at Our Cabaña becomes part of a Patrol and has a duty to do every day, just like at Pack Holiday! Girls can try Mexican crafts like silverwork, basketwork, leathercraft or pottery, and there is a swimming pool. As in all the Guide homes, there is a lot of singing and dancing at Our Cabaña.

The language spoken in Mexico is Spanish, so that is what most people speak at Our Cabaña. It's not a difficult language to learn:

Hola! means Hello.
¿Que tal? means How are you?
Por favor means Please.
¡Muchas gracias! means Thank you very much.

Mexican people are very polite. Even the poorest family expects visitors to shake hands with everyone when you arrive or say goodbye, and people always remember to say *Por favor* and *Gracias.*

PAX LODGE, ENGLAND

Pax Lodge is the newest of our World Centres, opened in London in 1990 by Princess Benedicte of Denmark, the Patron of the Olave Baden-Powell Society. A lot of the money to build and furnish it was raised by Brownies, Guides, Girl Scouts and leaders from all over the world – perhaps your Pack helped! Beside Pax Lodge there is the World Bureau, which is where WAGGGS 'lives'. Together, Pax Lodge and the World Bureau make up the Olave Centre.

Before Pax Lodge was opened we had a house in London which was first of all called 'Our Ark' and then became 'Olave House'. The dove in the Pax Lodge badge is shaped like an ark to remind us of the original World Centre called 'Our Ark'.

There are lots of meetings and training courses at Pax Lodge for Guides and Guiders and Girl Scouts from all over the world to get to know each other, find out about International Guiding and explore London.

SANGAM, INDIA

Sangam is in Pune, India. Its name is a Sanskrit word which means 'coming together' or 'joining together', so it is a good name for a place where many people come together and join together as friends!

When visitors arrive at Sangam they are given a garland of flowers and a pinch of salt to welcome them and ward off bad luck. Guests can try Indian crafts, learn how to tie saris and can try a traditional Maharashtrian dinner, dressed in Indian clothes and sitting on the floor using a banana leaf as a plate!

Sangam's buildings are built with many arches, and each arch represents opportunities opening up for the girls of the world. There is also a swimming pool to cool off in the humid weather.

At Sangam there are also special camps every year for Indian children who are not Guides or Scouts. When you are older you might be able to help at one of them. Even if you cannot visit Sangam, perhaps your Brownie Pack could raise some money to sponsor an Indian child on a camp – ask your Brownie Guider to write for the address of Sangam from the International Secretary at CHQ so that your Pack can write for details of how to sponsor a child on a Sangam camp.

Maybe one day you'll be able to visit one of our World Centre 'homes'!

EARLIEST, OLDEST AND FIRST

ICELAND

by Gillian Ellis   illustrated by Anna King

Ten facts to tell your friends

Did you know...

- the oldest recorded Parliament is the Alpingi of Iceland which began in AD 930?

- the earliest adhesive postage stamp in the world was the Penny Black, first sold on 1 May 1840?

- the oldest ruling house is that of Japan whose current Emperor is 125th in line from Jimmu Tenno the first ruler, believed to have ruled in the sixth century BC?

- the first man to set foot on the moon was an American, Neil Armstrong, on 21 July 1969?

- the oldest national flag is that of Denmark, dating from AD 1219? Its name is the Dannebrog, meaning 'Danish Cloth'.

- the oldest record in the BBC record library was made in 1884 and is of the Lord's Prayer?

- the first newspaper was printed in Sweden in 1644?

- the first controlled powered aircraft flight was made by an American, Orville Wright, on 17 December 1903?

- the oldest commercial airline still in business is KLM of the Netherlands, established in 1919 and first in service in May 1920?

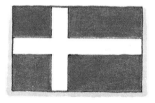

- the earliest known industry was 'flint knapping', which produced sharp tools for cutting and chopping made from a flaky stone called flint about 1,750,000 years ago?

The bear and the quicksand

an old story adapted by the Editor   illustrated by Kate Simpson

Tawny sighed. It had been a long day on Pack Holiday. First of all, Caroline had fallen out of bed at six o'clock in the morning and woken up the whole Pack. Then the Dolphins had got lost on the Treasure Hunt and by the time everybody had looked all over the woods for them, and found them, and walked back to the Pack Holiday Home, lunch was spoilt and late because the cooks hadn't been back in time. Then Sharon had been stung by a wasp. Then Rest Hour had been more like Rest Twenty Minutes because they had to catch the bus into town to go swimming. Frances had left her bag on the bus coming home and Brown Owl had had to drive to the garage to pick it up.

'Surely,' thought Tawny, as they trudged up the track to their house, 'nothing more can go wrong with today.' And just to prove her wrong, it started to rain. Kim, the Pack Leader, and Flipper, one of the Guiders, gritted their teeth and tried to get the Brownies to sing as they squelched their way home. But nobody felt like singing, so it was a damp and sad Brownie Pack that opened the door on their cosy home.

When they were all dried and changed they felt a bit better. Brown Owl showed them how to make scrunchies to tie their hair back. The Seahorses were cooks, so they went into the kitchen to help Flipper. The menu said fish fingers, baked beans and grilled tomato for tea, followed by a yogurt or a banana. So Nicky and Kathryn counted out yogurts and bananas, Sophie and Rachel stirred the baked beans in their enormous pan, and Frances cut up tomatoes to be grilled. Flipper unwrapped the fish fingers and began to put them carefully into a big frying pan.

Suddenly Kathryn yelped. 'A mouse!' she squeaked, as something dark streaked across the floor to hide under the cooker. At once the kitchen was in uproar. Kathryn and Nicky jumped up and down and squeaked. Sophie shot away across the room, while Rachel began to look

21

under the cooker. Frances dropped her knife and a tomato, got down on her hands and knees with Rachel and looked for the mouse.

Poor Flipper suddenly found herself with a Six of noisy, excited Brownies. Some of them wanted to catch the mouse, some of them didn't want to see it at all. Some of them were making a terrible din, some of them were crouched by the cooker with their faces almost on the ground, making squeaking noises to coax the mouse out. None of them were stirring the beans, or cutting the tomatoes, or putting out yogurts or bananas. The beans began to bubble and then to burn, the fish fingers to spit and frizzle and the tomatoes didn't do anything at all because Frances hadn't finished cutting them up.

'Help!' Flipper shouted. She didn't usually shout at all – she was very quiet and spoke to each Brownie individually, which they liked. Flipper's shout was such a surprise that they all looked at her. Even the mouse, safe under the cooker, looked up. 'Help!' said Flipper, more quietly.

'But, Flipper, there's a mouse!' said Rachel, reaching with a fork to see if she could get it out from under the cooker.

'Yes,' said Frances. 'Poor little thing, we want to take it outside.'

Rachel had her arm right under the cooker by this time. 'Bother!' she said. 'I think I'm stuck!' By this time Nicky had run into the other room to tell everyone what was happening, and all the rest of the Pack crowded into the kitchen to try and catch a glimpse of the mouse. Poor Flipper was suddenly swept away by Brownies. The tea was burning, the kettle was boiling, the yogurts were falling off the table and she was on the other side of the kitchen and couldn't do anything to stop them.

But among the Brownies who had run into the kitchen were Sammy and Priya. They looked round at the chaos and went into action. Quickly Priya turned off the gas under the bubbling, burning beans, the frizzling fish fingers and the kettle. Sammy picked up the knife and the tomato from the floor, and put the knife into the sink and the tomato into the waste bin. Priya stirred the beans to unstick them from the bottom of the pan and Sammy began to pick up the yogurts. Frances suddenly picked up the mouse and carried it outside, followed by almost all the Brownies – and

the kitchen was quiet again.

Flipper looked at Priya and Sammy. 'Thank you, you two,' she said.

Sammy said, 'Can we go and look at the mouse now, Flipper?'

'Yes,' said Flipper, 'but ask the Seahorses to come back, will you?'

And back came the Seahorses, and finished cooking the tea, and the mouse hid under a bush and thought about his narrow escape. But Tawny had been watching what had happened, and when the Pack were washed and changed and ready for bed, and sitting round the fire in the big room, she told them the story of the bear in the quicksand.

Once upon a time a bear went out for a walk. He reached a wide river with a wide sandy bank and began to walk along the sand, looking at the trees and the sky. But suddenly he felt a strange sucking sensation at his feet. He looked down and found that he was slipping into the soft wet sand.

"I know what this is," he thought. "It's quicksand! How can I get out?" Struggling and squirming he tried to pull out his feet, but it was no good – he just slipped further and further in.

"Help!" he cried. "Please help me!" A monkey

swung out of a tree and landed on a rock.

"I'm stuck in the quicksand!" cried the bear. "Please help me!"

"Help you?" said the monkey. "Didn't you know there was quicksand all along this river? You should have been more careful. It's your own fault." And he continued to tell the bear off, sitting on the rock.

Hearing the noise, a deer came through the trees. "What's going on?" he said.

"Please help me – I'm sinking in the quicksand!" begged the bear.

"Oh," said the deer. "I don't think there's anything I can do to help you. I think you had better prepare yourself to die. I know that's not a very nice thought, but try to be brave. Have you any messages for your relations? I once saw a squirrel stuck in this quicksand, and do you know what he said before he sank?" And the deer told the bear all about the squirrel at great length, and all the time the bear sank further into the quicksand.

Then a beaver came out of the woods. "What's happening?" she said.

The bear was up to his waist in the quicksand by now. "Please help get me out of this quicksand!" he cried. The beaver looked quickly about her. Then, choosing a tree close to the edge of the sands she began to gnaw through the trunk with her sharp front teeth. It took a few minutes, but soon the tree fell down, close to where the bear was stuck.

"Pull yourself on to the tree!" called the beaver to the bear. So the bear got hold of the tree and tried to heave himself on to it. He could feel the muscles in his arms and back almost bursting as he pulled and heaved – but at last he managed to pull himself out of the sand and along the tree trunk to the bank. There he lay, while the beaver brought him some water to drink and helped to clean some of the sand off him.

When he had got his breath back, he thanked the beaver very much. But he said to the deer and the monkey, "If it hadn't been for the beaver I'd have been dead by now. All you could do was talk – you wouldn't help me." He thanked the beaver again, turned around and began his walk home.

When he had gone, the beaver looked at the deer and the monkey. "When someone needs help," she said, "don't talk. Do something."

And even though the Brownies were really tired, they still knew what Tawny meant.

Meet the napkin gang!

by Jane Wilson   illustrated by Jane Hibbert

They're a colourful bunch and guaranteed to liven up a party or a special meal. You could make all the napkins the same for a party with a theme or make different characters to suit each of your guests. No need to stick to the ideas shown here – once you've learnt the basic method just let your imagination run riot and enrol lots more members of the napkin gang!

You will need:

Coloured paper napkins
Tracing paper
Soft pencil
White paper
Crayons or felt-tipped pens
Scissors
Glue

First select the design you want to use and trace it. Turn the tracing over and go over all the lines again with the soft pencil. Turn the tracing over again and place on the white paper and go over all the lines once more – this will mark the design on the white paper. (If you prefer you can photocopy the design directly from the *Brownie Guide Annual*. Photocopying machines can be found in most libraries and office stationery shops and copies usually cost about 10 pence each.) Colour in the character in any way you wish and then cut it out and follow the instructions to complete your chosen design.

WITCH

*Cut along the line between the brim of the hat and the band as far as the witch's head on both sides so that the brim will remain flat when the band is folded. Fold a black napkin using method **A**. Fold the band around the napkin about 6cm below the point and secure with a dab of glue.*

FATHER CHRISTMAS

*Fold a red napkin using method **A**. Fold the band around the napkin about 6cm below the point and secure with a dab of glue.*

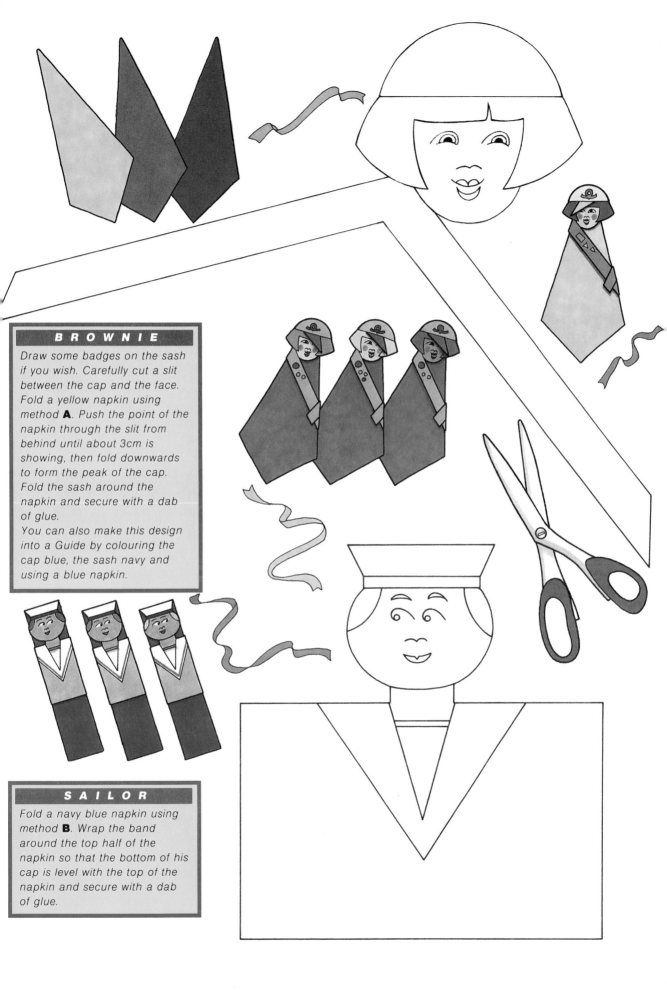

BROWNIE

Draw some badges on the sash if you wish. Carefully cut a slit between the cap and the face. Fold a yellow napkin using method **A**. Push the point of the napkin through the slit from behind until about 3cm is showing, then fold downwards to form the peak of the cap. Fold the sash around the napkin and secure with a dab of glue.

You can also make this design into a Guide by colouring the cap blue, the sash navy and using a blue napkin.

SAILOR

Fold a navy blue napkin using method **B**. Wrap the band around the top half of the napkin so that the bottom of his cap is level with the top of the napkin and secure with a dab of glue.

SOLDIER

Fold a black napkin using method **B**. Wrap the band around the top half of the napkin so that the bottom of his cap is level with the top of the napkin and secure with a dab of glue.

CHEF

Fold a white napkin using method **B**. Wrap the band around the top half of the napkin so that the bottom of his hat is level with the top of the napkin and secure with a dab of glue.

Napkin folds

Method A: Fold the napkin into three diagonally and turn over.
Method B: Place a pencil on each side of the napkin and roll them towards each other, rolling the napkin around them, until they meet in the centre. Secure the band before removing the pencils.

26

HOW'S YOUR GENERAL KNOWLEDGE?

by Heather Welford

Get those thinking caps on and try our quiz, by yourself or as a game between friends. Some questions are easy, some are fiendishly hard – either way, there's something for everyone!

THE WORLD

1 What is the name of the waterway between Great Britain and France?
2 Bombay, Delhi, Madras and Calcutta are big cities in which country?
3 What do we call a piece of land surrounded by sea?
4 Tokyo is the capital city of:
   a) China b) Canada c) Japan d) Peru
5 In which country do people speak Dutch?

THE BODY

1 What is the name of the dark circle on your eyeball?
2 How many digits do you have on your hands?
3 How many lungs do we have?
4 What are your 'milk teeth'?
5 What bit of you is sore if you have laryngitis?

BOOKS AND STORIES

1 Who lost her glass slipper at midnight?
2 Who wrote *The Twits*?
3 What was Jill Tomlinson's baby owl Plop afraid of?
4 Who climbed up the beanstalk?
5 Which magical country is reached through the back of the wardrobe?

ANIMALS, BIRDS AND INSECTS

1 What do we call a young goose?
2 How many legs has a fly?
3 What does a caterpillar become?
4 Which bird lays its eggs in other birds' nests?
5 Which animal is known as 'the king of the jungle'?

ANYTHING GOES

1 What colour medals are used for first, second and third in the Olympic games?
2 What is the name of the toy that looks like a tube, and inside one end has mirrors, beads and glass?
3 What is the name of Mickey Mouse's girlfriend?
4 Who was the famous English playwright born at Stratford on Avon?
5 You need a racquet to play badminton – but what is the name of the funny-looking object you hit with it?

The answers are on page 61.

Pieces of EIGHT

by Gillian Ellis   illustrated by Helen Herbert

Daisy was ill. She felt simply terrible. 'It's not fair!' she wailed miserably. 'I've been looking forward to Pack Holiday for ages!' Her mum hugged her.

'It's a shame,' she agreed. 'But you must just grin and bear it. There'll be other chances.' Daisy began to cry.

'I *can't* bear it!' she sobbed. 'And I never felt less like *grinning* in my life!'

'I'll fetch some juice,' said Mum. 'And a hanky.'

On Saturday, Daisy felt worse. Her head was made of wool, her legs of jelly, and she itched all over. She pictured the Brownies gathering at the coach and wept hopelessly. Nothing anyone said was any use.

'Here, Daisy,' offered Peter. 'You can help me with my model.'

'Hate models,' sulked Daisy.

'Shall I read to you?' suggested Frances. 'You can help me with the hard words.'

'No, thanks,' mumbled Daisy.

'How about a game of draughts?' said Dad. Daisy burrowed under the bedclothes and didn't even answer.

By Sunday, Daisy felt a little better. On Monday morning, she was able to go downstairs, though she seemed to have borrowed someone else's legs.

'I'm sorry I was horrid,' she said. 'I'll play games now. I just didn't feel like it before.'

That afternoon, Peter had a Scout hike and Frances was playing at her friend's house, so Daisy and Mum were alone. As they were settling down to watch TV, Daisy heard a noise in the hall. Mum went to investigate and came back with a parcel.

'It's for you,' she said. '*By Hand. Miss D Jones, Pugwash Crew.*'

Daisy was excited. 'Pugwash!' she exclaimed. 'That's the Six I would have been in!' She seized the parcel eagerly and tore open the paper. On top lay a letter, the strangest Daisy had ever seen.

'Look!' she said, puzzled. 'Half of it's pictures. I can't make head nor tail of it!'

'I used to do those,' said Mum. 'You have to work out the picture clues to read the letter. Let's do it together.' When she understood the message, Daisy's face was a picture itself!

'I can share the Holiday even if I can't be there!' she exclaimed. 'Brown Owl...I mean Long John Silver!...is brilliant!'

She rummaged in the parcel and found an assortment of fabric, card, glue and crayons. The afternoon passed in a flash. By teatime, Daisy had made a pirate hat, cutlass, eye patch and red-spotted triangular headscarf. She'd solved a pirate wordsearch, coloured in a Jolly Roger picture and begun a parrot mobile.

Daisy waited eagerly for the post next day. Sure enough, a thick package dropped on the mat. She set to work on the contents straight away. First there was a Treasure Island Map with clues. Each answer was the name of a place: 'Smugglers' Cove', 'Pretty Bay', 'Lookout Hill', and as Daisy solved each clue, she had to stick a tiny skull-and-crossbones flag on the map. Another picture letter told her how to make a Pugwash flag, and when Dad came home from work, he found it flying over the front door!

Daisy enjoyed her daily parcel so much, she hardly noticed herself getting better. On Thursday, when the Pack was due home, a letter arrived, all in code. Daisy was mystified, but Peter took one look and grinned.

'Easy-peasy!' he said. 'Just write the alphabet backwards.' Daisy couldn't think what he meant, but obediently wrote:
ZYXWVUTSRQPONMLKJIHGFEDCBA.

She studied it hard, then suddenly had an idea. Soon she had decoded the message and ran to obey it. Daisy found the box where the message had said it would be, and quickly spread its contents on the kitchen table.

'I've put the oven on at Mark 5,' said her mum. 'Call me when they're ready to bake.' Daisy mixed the ingredients thoroughly and rolled small balls of the mixture between her palms.

The morning raced by. At lunchtime heaps of crunchy golden biscuits lay cooling on wire racks and a delicious smell wafted through the house.

'Pieces of Eight!' grinned Daisy happily. 'Enough for a whole pirate crew!' There was still an hour till the Pirate Party which had been planned for the returning Brownies – time for the girls to dress up. Daisy wore the pirate hat and Frances the red headscarf. Peter looked on in amusement.

'Kids!' he scoffed, but he secretly thought it looked fun. The coach arrived at exactly two o'clock and a crowd of pirates tumbled out waving cutlasses. Long John Silver gave Daisy a hug.

'Better?' she asked, and Daisy nodded.

'Thanks ever so much for the parcels!' she said. 'I loved them. It was the next best thing to being there.'

'That's what I thought,' said Long John Silver. 'And now, me hearties...where are the Pieces of Eight?' The Pirate Party in Daisy's back garden was lovely. The Pieces of Eight went down well with Ship's Grog, served from the brass bucket which usually sat on Daisy's hearth. Pirate flags flew from the yard-arm (Mum's rotary drier) and the holiday ended with games on the lawn.

That night Daisy snuggled into bed, tired out but satisfied. 'I really was able to join in, thanks to Long John Silver,' she thought, happily. 'I think I must belong to the best Brownie Pack in the world.'

Here are Daisy's Pirate Puzzles. Can you solve them?

The answers to the puzzles are on page 61.

Pieces of Eight

You too can enjoy Pieces of Eight biscuits like Daisy and the rest of the pirate gang. Just follow this recipe!

Ingredients:
100g self-raising flour
100g rolled oats
1 teaspoon mixed spice
50g butter or margarine
100g sugar
2 tablespoons golden syrup

Method:
1 Mix the flour, oats and spice.
2 Melt the butter, sugar and syrup and pour over the dry mixture.
3 Mix thoroughly to a not-too-sticky consistency.
4 Dust your hands in flour and roll the mixture into walnut-sized balls.
5 Flatten the balls slightly between your palms and place them about 5cm apart on a lightly greased baking tray.
6 Bake for 8–10 minutes at 375°F, or 190°C, or Gas Mark 5 until golden brown.
7 Allow the biscuits to stand for five minutes and then transfer them to cooling trays.

STARS IN THE SKY!

by the Editor
illustrated by Jane Hibbert

Twinkle, twinkle, little star,
How I wonder what you are...

Everyone knows the old nursery rhyme, but how many of you know that the stars have names? The stars are millions of miles away from us – and from each other – but from where we are they look as if they are arranged in patterns, and over thousands of years we have given the shapes special names and told stories about them.

The shapes, or *constellations*, have names in Latin, like Ursa Major, Ursa Minor, Gemini, Cygnus and Leo, but many of them also have English names or nicknames. So Ursa Major becomes the Great Bear, Ursa Minor becomes the Little Bear, Gemini becomes the Twins and Cygnus the Swan. Some constellations are named after people in stories – Orion, Perseus or Cassiopeia.

Here are two legends from ancient Greece about constellations we can see in the skies over the United Kingdom.

ORION

Orion was a mighty hunter of ancient Greece, who was so good-looking that he was loved by the goddess Artemis. One day they went hunting on the island of Crete. Orion was hot and dusty, so he put down his spear and went for a swim in the sea.

Now Apollo the sun-god, who loved Artemis and was jealous of Orion, was watching, and when Artemis came out of the forest, he said to her, 'You may be a good hunter, but I bet you can't hit a moving target!'

Of course Artemis took up his challenge. 'Oh yes, I can!' she said. 'Which target?' Apollo shone and shone, so that Orion's head, above the waves, looked like a tiny dot. 'There it is,' he said. 'That mark out there in the sea.'

Artemis took up her bow and fitted an arrow to the string. She took careful aim – and fired. The arrow flew straight and true and hit the target. 'There,' she said. 'Who can't hit a moving target?' Apollo said nothing, but smiled to himself.

The hours passed. Artemis became puzzled, because Orion didn't come. The tide came in – and with it Orion's body, Artemis' own arrow in his head.

Artemis was beside herself with grief. She shook her fist at Apollo, and cried a great many tears, but there was nothing she could do. At last, she had an idea – one which would show Apollo just how important Orion had been to her. She took Orion up into the sky and put him there, with stars at his shoulders and knees, three stars at his belt and two along his sword.

And there (they say) he is even now, and if you look carefully on a dark night, you can see the stars outlining Orion.

Sir

THE PLEIADES

The Pleiades were seven sisters, daughters of Atlas, who carried the world on his shoulders. Their names were Maia, Taygete, Electra, Alcyone, Celoeno, Sterope and Merope. They were all beautiful and were loved by the gods, all expect Merope, who was loved by Sysiphus, a mortal man.

One day they were out walking when Orion saw them and began to chase them. They were

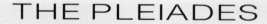

32

terrified and ran as fast as they could, but still Orion followed them. At last they cried out to Zeus, the kings of the gods, to help them.

Zeus looked out of the sky, and saw that the sisters could not run any further and Orion was just about to catch them. So he turned them all into doves, and they flew away, out of the reach of Orion. When they reached the sky, Zeus turned the doves into stars, and now they shine

know how to find North without a compass, and one way is to use the stars. At the very end of the tail of the Little Bear (Ursa Minor), there is quite a bright star, which hangs nearly over the North Pole. It's called the North Star or the Pole Star, or Polaris, and is quite easy to find.

Look into the sky until you see a constellation that looks like this:

in the sky, and you can see them if you find Orion, then look above him and a bit to the right. Usually you can only see six of the stars – Merope, because her lover was only a mortal, shines a little less brightly than her sisters. The Pleiades become visible in May, and when the Ancient Greeks saw them, they believed that the sister-stars had come back to the sky to signal the start of the summer.

There are lots of stories about the stars – not just from Greece but from other places around the world. See if you can find a book in the library about how the stars got their names.

The stars are useful, too! Every Brownie should

This is the Great Bear (Ursa Major). It's also sometimes called the Plough, because it looks like an old-fashioned plough with a long handle and deep blade. Sometimes it is even called the Saucepan! The two stars at the end are called the pointers because, if you follow the line they make, you come to the North Star. And the way to the North Star is – North!

There's a lot more to find out about stars. Why not get a book out of the library and ask your Guider if you can go outside and look? Remember – wrap up warmly, and never go looking at stars on your own – always go with someone you trust.

Healthy
FUN!

by Gillian Ellis   illustrated by Helen Herbert

Brownies Keep Healthy. What does that mean to you? Do you think of health just as 'not being ill'? Or do you look upon it as something much more positive?

At your age, adults play a large part in looking after your well-being, but don't leave it all to them! There are many things you can do yourself to keep your body in good condition. Try this quiz to see if you are on the right tracks.

Do you eat plenty of:
a) fruit?
b) vegetables?
c) wholemeal bread?
d) chocolate bars?
e) biscuits?
f) sweets?

Do you regularly drink:
a) milk?
b) water?
c) fresh fruit juice?
d) cola?
e) sweetened fizzy pop?
f) sweetened cordial?

Do you spend most of your spare time:
a) playing outside?
b) practising a sport?
c) going for walks?
d) watching television?
e) playing computer games?
f) knitting or sewing?

Do you clean your teeth:
a) twice a day?
b) after breakfast and before bed?
c) after every meal?
d) once a day?
e) once a week?
f) once a year?

Do you brush your hair:
a) every morning and evening?
b) when it feels tangled?
c) when you know it's untidy?
d) only when you get up?
e) when your mum makes you?
f) when someone says it's a mess?

Do you go to bed early:
a) every night?
b) most nights?
c) weeknights, a bit later at weekends?
d) only occasionally?
e) only when your parents make you?
f) never?

If you can truthfully answer a), b) or c) to all or most of the questions, then you're well on the way to healthy living. Those with more than one or two d, e or f answers need to shape up a bit!

Try some of these lively outdoor games with your friends.

In pairs, try:

Danish Wrestling

With someone your own size, join right hands and face each other with right feet touching. Both try to make your opponent move her right foot by pulling, pushing or twisting. You can move your left feet as much as you like.

Knee Boxing

Both at the same time, try to touch your opponent's knees!

Shadow Tag

On a sunny day, try to step on each others' shadow without your opponent stepping on yours.

In fours, try:

Prisoner!

One player stands in the middle of a circle made by the other three with hands joined. No other parts of the body must touch. The 'prisoner' tries to escape from the circle while the rest try to stop her.

Touch the Target

One player, the chaser, stands outside a circle made by the others, hands joined. She names one person, who is the 'target', and counts to five while the circle moves round so that the target is as far away from the chaser as possible. The chaser tries to touch the target by running round the outside while the circle tries to prevent this by spinning round. The chaser changes places with the target when she catches her.

In fives or sixes, try:

Snake's Tail

Stand in line, arms round each others' waists. The front player, who is the snake's head, tries to catch the last player, the snake's tail. The snake must not break in two.

You should have some colour in your cheeks when you've played these energetic games!

If you go down to the woods today...
...be sure to take a

Teddy bears'
picnic

written and photographed by Jane Wilson

Even if it's only in the back garden or your bedroom, teddies love a picnic and so do young children. A teddy bears' picnic would be a lovely way for a Brownie to entertain younger brothers, sisters, cousins or friends and do a good turn by giving their mum a bit of a rest!

Just prepare some of the teddy-sized food suggested here (or think of some of your own) and pack it into a small bag. You'll need an adult to help you with the things you cook. An insulated lunch pack would make an ideal teddy's cold bag, or you could use a small basket or hamper. Add some small plates and beakers, napkins and a tablecloth for a posh picnic and head for the great outdoors.

TEDDY OGGIES

Put the minced beef and onion into a saucepan and cook over a gentle heat, stirring all the time, until the mince is just brown.

Add the potato and carrot cubes to the pan and crumble in the beef stock cube. Pour on just enough water to cover the bottom of the pan, put a lid on and cook for about ten minutes, stirring occasionally.

When the vegetables are just soft, take the pan off the heat and leave to cool.

Cut the margarine and lard into lumps and put into a mixing bowl with the flour. Gently rub the fat and flour between your fingers, lifting it into the air as you do, until the mixture looks like fine crumbs.

Stir in the water, a little at a time, until the mixture makes a stiff dough. Gather it into a ball.

Sprinkle flour on to a work surface and rolling pin and roll the pastry out until it is about 3mm thick. Using a large round cutter (about 9cm), cut out circles of pastry. Gather up the leftover pastry, roll it again and cut more circles until the pastry is used up.

Put a heaped teaspoonful of the meat and vegetable mixture in the centre of each circle of pastry. Brush the edges of the pastry with water. Fold the pastry into a semi-circle, with the edges on top, and pinch them together firmly.

Put the teddy oggies on a baking tray which has been greased or lined with baking parchment. Cook at 180°C (350°F, Gas Mark 4) for about 20 minutes, until they are golden brown.

200g minced beef
1 small onion, finely chopped
1 small potato, peeled and cut into small cubes
1 large carrot, peeled and cut into small cubes
1 beef stock cube
200g plain flour
50g margarine
50g lard or white vegetable fat
50ml water (approx)

McTED'S EGGS

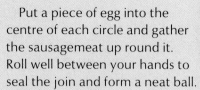

1 hard-boiled egg
250g sausagemeat
30g golden breadcrumbs

Peel the egg and cut it into quarters. Divide each quarter into three, so that you have twelve pieces altogether.

Divide the sausagemeat into twelve pieces and flatten them into circles.

Put a piece of egg into the centre of each circle and gather the sausagemeat up round it. Roll well between your hands to seal the join and form a neat ball.

Put the breadcrumbs on to a plate and roll each ball in them until it is coated all over.

Place the balls on a baking tray and cook at 180°C (350°F, Gas Mark 4) for about 20 minutes.

PAW-SIZE PASTA

50g tiny pasta shapes (often sold as pasta for soup)
50g sweetcorn, tinned or frozen
A few chives
50g cherry tomatoes

Bring about 200ml water to the boil in a small saucepan. Add the pasta and cook for about 5 minutes until it is soft but still chewy. Carefully tip the pasta into a sieve, pour some cold water over it, then cover and leave it to drain and cool.

Put the cooled pasta into a bowl with the sweetcorn. Hold the chives over the bowl and snip them into short lengths using kitchen scissors. Cut the tomatoes into quarters, add to the bowl and stir everything together.

FURRY CAKES

50g soft margarine
50g caster sugar
1 egg
50g self-raising flour
30g butter
30g drinking chocolate
10g desiccated coconut
About 20 'petit four' cases (miniature paper cake cases)

Put the margarine and sugar into a bowl and cream together until they are soft and fluffy.

Beat the egg in a cup, then gradually beat it into the margarine and sugar.

Sift the flour and stir it gently into the bowl.

Spread the paper cases out on a baking tray and place one teaspoon of mixture in each case. Cook at 180°C (350°F, Gas Mark 4) for about ten minutes until the cakes are golden brown on top and springy to touch.

Put the cakes on a wire rack and allow to cool.

To make the icing, cream the butter and drinking chocolate together, then stir in the desiccated coconut. Spread a little icing on each of the cooled cakes.

HONEYBEAR SCONES

100g *self-raising flour*
20g *margarine*
1 tablespoon *runny honey*
50ml *milk*

Cut the margarine into lumps and put into a mixing bowl with the flour. Gently rub the margarine and flour between your fingers, lifting it into the air as you do, until the mixture looks like fine crumbs.

Add the honey and milk to the bowl and stir until you have a soft dough.

Turn out on to a floured work surface and roll the dough out to about 1cm thick. Using a small round pastry cutter (about 4cm across) cut out circles of dough. If you have not got a small cutter perhaps you could use an egg cup or sherry glass, but be sure to ask permission first. Gather up the leftover dough, re-roll and cut more circles until it is used up.

Place the scones on a baking tray which has been greased or lined with baking parchment and cook at 180°C (350°F, Gas Mark 4) for about ten minutes, until they are golden brown on top.

Put the scones on a wire rack and leave to cool. The cooled scones can be split in half and spread with butter.

Don't worry if you haven't got time to make all or any of these recipes – these teddies are having an excellent picnic with things that can be made very quickly or bought ready made. Here are some ideas:

- Make sandwiches with thin-sliced bread and cut them into squares about 3cm across.
- Cut an individual pork pie or quiche into six or eight wedges.
- Some brands of biscuits, both savoury and sweet, can be bought in miniature versions, usually sold in small bags.
- Make a small jelly in an individual mould or an old carton from an ice-cream or mousse.
- A mini swiss roll can be cut into slices as if it were a full-sized version.
- Bunches of tiny seedless grapes are ideal for small hands and paws, and healthy too.
- Miniature bars of chocolate are a treat for teddies and children alike!

Moving ON

by Gillian Ellis   Illustrated by Helen Herbert

Helen loved Brownies. Even when she was nearly eleven, and all her friends were going up, she flatly refused to move to Guides.

'If I can't stay in Brownies, I'm leaving,' she said. 'I just don't fancy Guides.'

Helen wouldn't listen when Tawny tried to tell her she'd love Guides. How could she, when she felt so shy? The Guides looked enormous, and she hardly knew them. So when her friends went up, Helen stayed behind, ashamed to admit how scared she was.

After three weeks, Vicky and Lisa came back to visit the Pack.

'Guides is fantastic!' Vicky said. 'We're making kites.'

'My Patrol went hiking,' added Lisa. 'We made a fire and cooked sausages. We got filthy but it was great!'

'Can we, Brown Owl?' asked Jennifer eagerly.

'Sorry, Jennifer, no,' said Brown Owl. 'Wait till you're a Guide. It's more fun to plan it yourself.' There was a general groan, but Helen was relieved because she thought fire-lighting sounded rather scary.

Early in May, Helen's cousin invited her to an 'adventure party' for her thirteenth birthday. 'Come in old clothes,' she said. Helen was very excited. On the day, she scrambled into her oldest jeans and jumper and went eagerly to Jane's.

When she got there, Helen couldn't see any signs of a party. There was no food out and she couldn't hear any music. The other girls were all older than she was, and she felt shy. Everyone was asking about the 'adventure' so Jane's mum explained.

'You're pioneers on a Waggoners' Trail,' she said, 'trekking to California in search of gold. On the journey you'll meet some problems, but there'll be some friendly Indians to help you. Your wagon's in the garden and you'll be living in it for months, so make it comfy. That's your first task.' She handed Jane a card and the girls crowded round eagerly.

The card began a trail of clues leading to hiding places where the girls found coloured counters and Scrabble letters which they had to arrange into a word. Helen was good at anagrams and quickly worked it out...TOOLSHED. There, in a flowerpot, they found a whistle, labelled 'Indians'. Jane handed it to Helen.

'You solved the clue,' she said, 'you can give the signal.'

Helen blew hard. Nothing happened.

'Try lots of little blows,' suggested Jane. This time a grinning 'Indian' appeared – Helen's Uncle Pete, wearing a feather head-dress and carrying groundsheets, sleeping-bags and blankets, which he solemnly 'sold' for the counters. Soon the wagon was full of beds.

The next task was to find food! The girls followed signs made with twigs and stones. Jane showed Helen and Anna, a girl who seemed to be nearer Helen's age, what they meant. Helen enjoyed herself, all shyness gone. The other girls were nice, especially the one called Linda.

The bag of food was up a tree and there seemed to be no way of reaching it, so Helen whistled for the Indian again. Silently, he produced a long stick and pulled down a rope-ladder from the branches.

'I love rope-ladders!' said Anna. She climbed up carefully and brought down the bag. Helen peered inside. 'Raw meat!' she said, astonished, and Jane giggled.

'And matches!' she said. 'Seems we cook our own tea!' Jane showed Helen how to take dead wood from the trees in her garden, then Linda built a fire on a bare patch of ground. Helen thought it was clever the way she piled twigs into a neat pyramid and positioned logs to hold the frying pan. Helen had a turn at cooking sausages and kebabs, and the Indian brought ice-cream.

Next, the Waggoners had to solve a code-message, which led them to the garden pond, where the Indian helped them make balsa-wood boats. Finally an obstacle course brought them to the gold – foil-covered chocolate money!

Helen couldn't believe how fast the party went.

'I've had a great time,' she said. 'I liked the cook-out best.'

Linda said casually, 'We're having another in my garden, Tuesday evening. Like to come?' Helen was thrilled.

'Love to,' she said, so Jane promised to call for her.

Helen couldn't wait for Tuesday. At Linda's, now that she knew everyone, Helen felt quite at home. She helped lay the fire, and Linda let her light it. They had soup and beefburgers, eating them sitting round the embers. Linda was teaching them silly songs which made Helen giggle, when she heard a familiar voice.

'Glad you decided to join, Helen,' said Brown Owl.

Helen stared. 'How d'you mean, join?' she said.

'Oh, sorry,' grinned Linda. 'Didn't I mention this was our Patrol meeting? I meant to.'

'Patrol?' said Helen, astonished. 'Guides?'

'Every so often,' Linda explained, 'Patrols meet on their own. Next week you'll come to the Hut — if you want to, that is. You can be in Swallows. We're making sweets next Tuesday. How about it?'

Suddenly Helen liked the idea very much. It would be good in Linda's Patrol.

'I'll be there,' she said, wondering why she'd ever been shy of the older girls.

After she had gone home, Brown Owl grinned at the Guides. 'Thanks, Swallows,' she said. 'Your adventure party seems to have done the trick! Jane, give your parents my thanks for their help. By the way, send me a peppermint cream at Brownies — via Helen!'

CASTLES AND ROSES

by Gillian Ellis   illustrated by Jane Hibbert

Canals look so much part of the landscape in some places that it's easy to forget that they haven't always been there. But before there were trains and lorries to transport coal and food and wood and all the other things people needed to live, it was much easier to move things about by boat, and many ports grew up around our rivers and coasts.

But not everyone lives close to the coast and boats couldn't sail up some rivers, so when the Industrial Revolution came, and factories and mills were built in many places inland, artificial rivers called canals were built so that goods made in one place could be moved cheaply and fairly quickly to be sold in another.

The canals were not very wide and were built in fairly straight lines with very gentle curves so that the boats slipped along them easily. The boats that went on canals were long and thin – they were (and still are) called narrowboats, and were often only two metres across, so that they could meet and pass each other on the canal.

But a narrowboat wasn't just a container for moving goods from one place to another. It was also a home for the bargee and often large families lived in the tiny cabin – maybe only the size of a small bedroom.

Narrowboat wives were very proud of their homes and their boats were kept in very good order. Inside and out the boats were painted in bright colours, with castles and roses of red, yellow and green. In fact, everything the family owned was painted in the same way, right down to the kettle and the bucket used for mopping the deck. The narrowboat's name was painted on the front and back and the owner's name on the side.

The cabins were crammed with decorations such as painted china wallplates, often interlaced with ribbons, and pieces of lace and crochetwork. Lots of folding furniture meant that a tiny cabin could house a cooking range, cupboard, table, seats and bed.

The boats didn't have engines at first, so how did they move? A horse was harnessed up to a long tow-rope, and along the side of the canal there was a path – still called a towpath, even on modern canals – and the horse

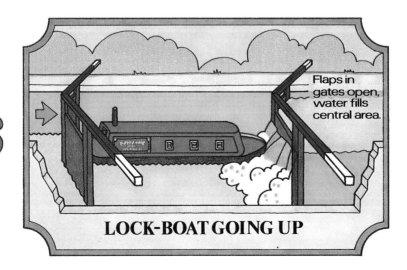

Flaps in gates open, water fills central area.

LOCK-BOAT GOING UP

plodded along that, pulling the boat behind it. Because it's much easier to pull something along the water than on the ground, the horse could easily pull even a heavily laden barge.

When the canal came to a hill, sometimes there would be a deep cutting through the top of the hill if it was a low one, or there would be a narrow tunnel. Usually there wasn't a towpath, so one member of the family would take the horse to the other end of the tunnel and wait, while the bargee and other members of the family would get the boat through the tunnel by lying on their backs on the cabin roof and 'walking' along the top of the tunnel overhead. This was called 'legging', and must have been very hard work!

Sometimes, though, the narrowboat would go up and down hills by using a clever system of locks. A lock is a stretch of water in the canal with a 'gate' at each end. At one end of the lock, the gate is closed and outside it the water level is high. In the lock, the water level is much lower, and the other gate is open. A boat travelling up the lock enters the lock at the low end, and the gate is closed behind it. Gradually water is let in at the 'high' end, and as the lock fills up and the water level rises, the boat floats higher and higher. When the water level inside the lock is the same as the level outside the gate, the gate is opened and the boat can continue its journey.

The same sort of thing happens when a boat travelling the other way wants to go 'downhill'. This time the lock has to be full of water before the boat goes in and when the 'high' gate has been closed behind the boat, water is let out gradually at the 'low' end. When the boat is at the same level as the water outside the 'low' gate, it is opened and the boat travels on. Often there are lots of locks up a long hill, just like a staircase, and getting a boat from one end to the other can take a long time!

At one time canals were very important to the industry of Great Britain (did you know that Birmingham has more canals than Venice?) but when railways were built goods could be transported greater distances much more quickly than by water, and canals fell out of use. Many were blocked up or filled in, and only a few people cared for them.

Nowadays, though, some people still live in narrowboats, and even more people enjoy holidays on canal boats, although most boats today have engines instead of horses! Many canals have been restored by people who love them, and there are museums in some places where you can see canal boats and find out more about how barge families live and worked.

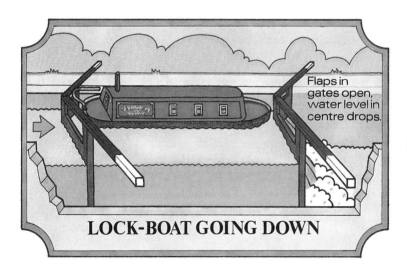

Flaps in gates open, water level in centre drops.

LOCK-BOAT GOING DOWN

eggs-*amining* eggs!

by Gill Pawley
illustrated by Anna King

Do you like eggs? Even if you are not too keen on ordinary eggs, most Brownies love chocolate Easter eggs! These pages are all about eggs – things to make and do, and some egg-citing facts.

EGG-STREMELY NICE SANDWICHES

One of the nicest things you can make with eggs is an egg sandwich.

You will need:
2 eggs
bread
butter or margarine
salt and pepper
a small pan
a small bowl and a fork
help from an adult

You need to hard-boil the eggs first, so you must ask an adult to help you to do this.

1 Put a small pan of water on to boil, and when it is boiling away, put one egg into a tablespoon and gently lower it into the water, then do the same with the other.

2 Bring the water back to the boil and let it boil gently for 8–9 minutes. Then turn off the heat.

3 Carefully lift the pan off the ring and put it in the sink. Run cold water into the pan until the shells are cool enough to touch. Then lift them out and tap them gently on a hard surface to crack the shell and peel it off.

4 While the eggs are still warm, put them into a small dish and use a fork to mash them with a little butter and some salt and pepper.

5 Butter the bread, then spread the egg mixture on one of the slices. If you have some cress, add some of that, too!

6 For really posh sandwiches, cut off the crusts and serve on a china plate.

Look in a recipe book for other recipes using eggs and try some of them – perhaps on Pack Holiday!

Do you know that a fresh egg sinks in water, while a rotten egg floats? This is because a fresh egg has a small space at one end with air in it between the shell and the membrane (a sort of bag containing the yolk and the white). Because eggs are denser than water, they sink, but because water is heavier than air, the end of the egg with the air space points upwards and the egg stands on its end. As an egg gets older, the air space gets bigger and spreads out, so when the egg is put into water, the amount of air in it makes it float!

Eggs are traditional at Easter, because they are a symbol of new life – from cold, round, hard eggs are born tiny, fluffy little chickens, ducklings and other birds. Christians believe that Jesus died on a cross and then became alive again, so they give eggs to each other to celebrate this and to be a reminder of Jesus breaking out of his tomb. Nowadays, most people give eggs made of chocolate!

'Pace-egging' is an Easter event in some places in the north of England. Children paint eggs and then roll them down a slope. The winner is the one whose egg goes furthest without breaking.

It is also traditional at Easter time to decorate hard-boiled eggs in some way – perhaps by painting faces on them or making patterns with wax and dye.

DON'T TOUCH

Did you know that collecting birds' eggs is against the law? Some birds are specially protected in the breeding season to stop egg collectors stealing their eggs and so stopping baby birds being born.

EGG-STRAORDINARY

- The biggest eggs in the world are laid by the ostrich and are usually 15–20cm long and 10–15cm wide. They weigh around 1.7kg (a bit less than two bags of sugar!) and take 40 minutes to boil!
- The smallest eggs in the world are laid by the Vervain hummingbird from Jamaica. They are less than 1cm long and weigh less than one gramme – very tiny indeed!
- The largest omelette ever made contained 54,763 eggs and 240kg cheese. It was cooked in a pan 9.1 metres in diameter in the USA in 1986.
- In 1982, Siegfried Berndt of the 'Macopa' patisserie in Leicester made an Easter egg which was 3 metres high and weighed 347.7kg!
- The longest distance an egg has ever been thrown between two people without breaking is 96.9 metres.
- The record number of yolks in a hen's egg is nine – found in an egg laid by a hen on a farm in New York State.

And here's another 'yolk'...
Why are cooks cruel?
Because they beat eggs!

S-EGG-REGATION

If you're cooking with more than one egg, it's a good idea to break them one at a time into a cup before adding them to the mixture. If one of the eggs is bad, it lands in the cup on its own, instead of in the mixture with all the other ingredients!

Crushed eggshells can be put around your favourite plants in the garden to keep off hungry slugs. This is because slugs are very soft underneath, and they don't like crawling across the sharp edges of the shells! You can also put broken eggshells on the compost heap.

If you fancy having a beady-
eyed barley buddy, why not
make our

froggy
friend

by the Editor
illustrated by Helen Herbert

You will need:

Thin, greaseproof or tracing paper and a pencil to trace
the patterns
Two pieces of fabric about the size of these two pages
Pins, needle and thread
A packet of barley (about 500g)
Two beads with holes through for eyes

1 Place a sheet of paper over the pattern on
the page opposite and draw around one of
the outlines – follow either the blue or the
red line when you get to the tummy.
Repeat with another sheet of paper, this
time following the other outline. Then cut
out the two shapes. These are your
patterns.

2 Fold one of your pieces of fabric so that the
wrong sides are together and pin the larger
pattern piece to it. Cut round the pattern
and remove the pins. Then fold the other
piece of fabric, but this time pin the pattern
to the fabric with the straight edge against
the fold, as shown. Cut round the shape,
remove the pins and unfold the fabric so
that you have a frog shape. This will be the
frog's tummy.

3 Take the two 'half-frog' shapes, lie them
right sides together and pin along the back.
Sew the back seam using back stitch. You
should now have a frog shape which won't
lie flat.

4 Lie the tummy piece flat, right side facing
upwards, and lie the other piece right side
down on top of it. Pin them together – the
top one won't lie flat so be careful to pin
round the very edges.

5 Using back stitch again, sew right round
the shape, starting at **A** and finishing at **B**
(see the letters on the pattern). Finish off
firmly.

6 Carefully turn the frog shape inside out.
Use the blunt end of a pencil to push out
the webbed hands and feet.

7 Carefully pour in some barley, a little at a
time (use a yogurt pot so you don't spill
too much!), until the frog is about half full.
Work the barley into the arms and head
and about half the body. Decide for
yourself whether you need any more
barley – it will depend on how floppy you
want your frog.

8 Carefully fold under the raw edges, pin and
oversew the hole.

9 Decide where you want the eyes to go,
and sew the beads in place. If you don't
have any beads, use felt circles.

10 Finally, shake the frog to spread the barley
out and give it a name!

You can sit your frog in all sorts of poses!

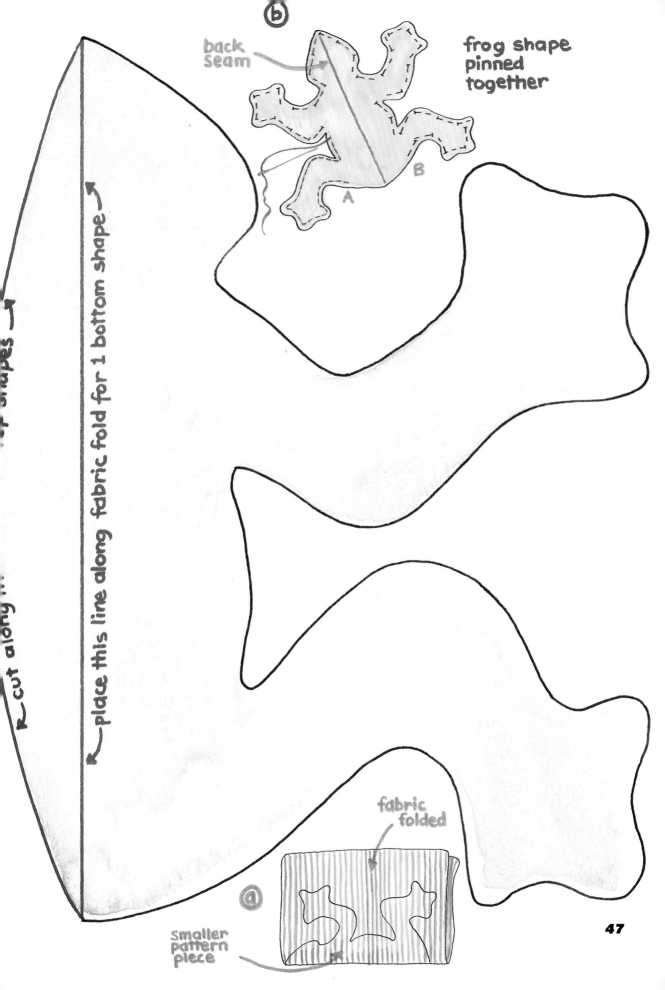

back
seam

frog shape
pinned
together

A

B

ⓑ

cut along the top shapes

place this line along fabric fold for 1 bottom shape

fabric
folded

ⓐ

smaller
pattern
piece

47

WHY THE CAT LIVES AT HOME

by Kiera Kindermann   illustrated by Gini Wade

A long time ago when jungles and forests covered the earth, the cat was a wild creature. She wandered alone in the long grasses and burning heat of the tropics. For her food she caught the tiny wild animals and for her drink she went down to the shady pools. But once upon a time there was one cat who changed all that.

To look at she was like any other wild cat. Her fur was short and shadowed with grey and white stripes. If she lay in the grass or under the bushes she became almost invisible.

Late one evening, before the sun had set, she went to the pool as usual. She drank quickly because there was nowhere for her to hide. Her dark stripy body stood out clearly against the white sand. While she bent her head to lap the cool water, a dark shadow flew overhead. It was a bird of prey looking for its dinner. When the huge bird dropped like a stone to take her in its claws, she saw its reflection in the water.

As the bird landed, the cat leapt to one side. She felt its breath and the brush of its feathers. She dived into the undergrowth and ran for her life.

At last, too tired to run any more, she crept into a hollow tree and listened. Nothing came crashing through the trees after her. Slowly she stopped panting and, tired out, fell asleep.

When she woke again she remembered the chase like a bad dream and shivered. 'I don't want to be dinner for another creature,' she thought. 'I

48

must find myself a friend. It must be a creature that will protect me from other wild animals.'

So she crept out of her hiding place and went to look for a friend. The first animal she met was a cat like herself. But this cat was huge. He had long shaggy hair around his face and when he roared the whole jungle shook. He was a lion. The little cat knew that lions did not eat their own relations. 'This is the friend for me,' she purred. So she strutted up to the lion, who was lying in the sun. She looked up into his hairy face and mewed loudly, 'Excuse me, Mr Lion.'

The lion swung his head lazily to look at her. 'Yes, little cousin. What can I do for you?'

'Please, Sir, you are the strongest and bravest animal of them all. I'm looking for a friend. Will you be my friend and protect me from the other wild creatures?'

The lion lifted his huge head and roared with laughter. 'Well, little cousin, if I agree to be your friend and protect you, what will you do for me in return?'

The little cat smiled shyly. 'I can comb your long mane with my claws and keep your fur clean.'

The lion lifted a large paw and scratched lazily. 'Yes,' he agreed, 'it would be good to get rid of these fleas. You may start at once!'

So the little cat set to work immediately. Every day she kept the lion groomed and stayed close to him. She even slept between his huge paws. She felt safe.

But one day, they met a herd of elephants. The lion watched a baby elephant wander away from its mother. He approached closer, thinking it might make a good dinner for that day. But the leader of the herd, the baby's old aunt, saw the lion creep through the long grasses. She raised her trunk in alarm and spread her giant ears.

While the lion crept closer to the baby, the elephant charged. She crashed through the bushes and picked up the lion in her great long tusks as if he was a toy. She tossed him in the air with an angry trumpeting roar. The lion turned over and over in the air and landed with a thump on the ground. He shook himself. The elephant thundered towards him again. The lion struggled up and ran for his life.

The little cat watched this from a safe distance. She said to herself, 'So the lion is not the strongest animal in the jungle. I must make friends with the elephant and ask her to protect me.'

She crept out of her hiding place and stole up to the elephant. She stood between the elephant's tree-trunk-like feet and mewed loudly.

'Excuse me, Mrs Elephant.'

The elephant looked down from her great height. 'Hello, little friend of the night! What can I do for you?'

'Oh, Mrs Elephant! You are the biggest and bravest animal in the jungle. You are even stronger and fiercer than the lion, who thinks he rules the other animals. Please will you be my friend and protect me from the creatures who want to eat me for their dinner?'

The elephant swung her trunk as she thought about this. 'If I help you,' she said slowly, 'what can you do to help me?'

The little cat purred. 'Oh, Mrs Elephant. I know how my cousins, the big cats, hunt. I can tell you when they are near so you can warn your babies. That is how I can help you.'

The elephant nodded her rock-like head slowly. 'Good, good,' she said in agreement. 'Yes, let us be friends.'

So the little cat stayed with the elephant, the leader of the herd. For a time, she was happy with her new friend.

One dark night there was a great panic in the herd. As the elephants stood dozing under the trees, men crept up with their bows and arrows. The men were not frightened as the leader charged with her huge ears spread and her trunk raised in anger. They shot her dead with many arrows. As the men took away the great body for their feast, the little cat crept out of the shadows. She stalked up to the leader of the hunting party.

'Oh, Sir!' she mewed boldly. 'I have seen brave creatures in this jungle fighting with other brave animals. But I have never seen any animal as brave as you. You indeed rule the jungle!'

The man stood with his hands on his hips and looked down at the little cat. 'Well, well, well,' he chuckled. 'What does a little animal like you want with me, the greatest creature in the jungle?'

'Oh, please, Sir,' she asked politely, 'will you be my friend and protect me from the other animals in the jungle?'

The man put his head on one side and thought for a moment. 'But why,' he asked, 'would I want you as my friend?'

'Ah!' answered the cat. 'I can see better than you in the dark. I could guide you through the jungle at night when you go hunting.'

'Why not?' laughed the man. 'Join our hunting party, little friend.'

So the cat led the men back through the jungle to their houses, which stood on top of a small hill.

The dawn sky was becoming silvery grey when the men arrived home. The little cat's new friend walked into his grass-thatched house and called to his wife.

His wife was in the kitchen. She ran out, her face hot with anger. 'Where have you been for a whole week? The children are starving. We have been living on leaves and roots! What kind of husband are you?'

As she shouted, the man started to back away into the corner.

'Call yourself a hunter? Bah! I could hunt better than you! Even the children catch more food than you do! You sleep and drink for weeks and then go out and catch a tough old elephant!'

The man cringed at her words. 'But, but, but,' he stammered, 'there was nothing in the jungle. All the animals have moved away.'

'See, you even frighten away the animals with your noise.'

The man crept out of his house while his wife threw harsh words after him. The little cat watched in amazement. 'Well,' she thought, 'if the bravest, strongest creature in the jungle is frightened of his wife, then she must be the greatest of them all!'

She walked up to the woman and bowed her head in respect. 'Oh, Madam, Madam! Please let me be your friend. I can chase the rats and mice away from your kitchen and your home, if only you will be my friend.'

The woman was surprised by this little creature. But she was a practical person. 'Yes,' she answered. 'I have a lot of rats and mice in my home. They eat our food. I need someone to chase them away. Yes, you can stay, if you keep them away.'

And so that is how the cat came to live with her new-found friend, the woman. And now many, many years later her great-great grandchildren still live in our homes. And they still almost always prefer the woman of the house.

```
C R T H A D C Z B U R A U N I X W V O F G P
P D I M W J X A I K W R W A D F S X H S A V
T O D M K X B U E Z L I T T L E F R I E N D
Q G H R A C F W N A G J L Y O V B Y X A A Z
Z L X A B L X A L I T A P L G T Z M T R N W
D U A E O F A R I M C K D L R I T E W E S L
R T Z O U W U D I S D E A P O U L I A Z E N
W I C H T E L T Y S O K J Z N S C S F T G Y
S N F H E C T Q K B K S P T S X P E A W U Z
P S T A R S C O U T I C X J M S U P O K I S
Y T X B L U E B I R D R Z B U L B U L Z D D
S O E E A K C S K T B O D E T W O F T L E P
N R W J E A N N E T T E P T T X K S R W O T
W L B A M D E M T M Z Y R T E C O L W A O E
```

Brownie friends competition

All over the world there are girls like you who are Brownies, but as you know they're not all called Brownies! On the right we have listed the names for Brownies in 18 countries. The same names are hidden in the wordsquare – all you have to do is find all 18 and put a ring around each one and then send:

◆ a photocopy of the page or a copy of the completed wordsquare
◆ your name, address and age
◆ the names of the three things you liked best in this year's Brownie Annual

to:

Brownie Friends
The Brownie Annual 1993
The Girl Guides Association
17-19 Buckingham Palace Road
London SW1W 0PT

The closing date is 31 January 1993.

Argentina – ALITA
Australia – WICHTEL
Belgium – LUTIN
Denmark – GRONSMUTTE
France – JEANNETTE
Ghana – ANANSE GUIDE
Greece – POULIA
India – BULBUL
Israel – OFARIM
Italy – LADYBIRD
Japan – BURAUNI
Netherlands – KABOUTER
Norway – MEISE
Philippines – STAR SCOUT
Sri Lanka – LITTLE FRIEND
Switzerland – BIENLI
Thailand – BLUEBIRD
Uruguay – ABEJA

The first three correct entries pulled out of the editor's hat will win a set of four Brownies around the World books. There will also be five prizes of a selection of Brownie goodies.

Good luck!

gift wrapping
IN THE BAG!

by Jane Wilson   photographs by Grant Wilson

If you hate wrapping presents, or you've got something to wrap up that's an awkward shape, these easy-to-make gift bags could be just the answer you're looking for.

The instructions tell you how to make a bag from half a sheet of wrapping paper, which will give a finished size of approximately 23cm x 26cm. A quarter of a sheet of paper will make a bag 15cm x 17cm, while an eighth of a sheet makes a bag 11cm x 12cm. To make these smaller bags simply follow the same instructions but make all the folds and overlaps slightly smaller.

You will need:

Half a sheet of wrapping paper
Glue
Ruler
Pencil
Hole punch
Ribbon or cord

1

With the paper in front of you so that it is wider than it is tall, fold down 4cm at the top and glue in place.

2

Using a ruler and pencil, mark the centre of the paper, then fold in each side to 1cm beyond the centre mark. Glue together where they overlap and allow the glue to dry.

4 ▶

Holding the bottom layer of this fold against the bag, open the top layer up again. This will leave two triangles of the patterned side of the paper showing against the white inside. Line up the creases down the centre of these with the fold at the bottom of the bag and crease firmly at the edges to hold in place.

3

Fold up 5cm at the bottom of the bag.

◀ **5**

Fold the top flap (with the glued seam) down to 1cm below the fold line and the bottom flap up to 1cm above the fold line. Open up again and look at the pattern made by the folded lines – you will see a small triangle at each end of the two flaps. Put a dab of glue on each triangle on the top flap and fold down. Glue the triangles and along the edge of the bottom flap and fold up. Allow the glue to dry.

6

Punch holes in the top edge of the bag, making sure that they are evenly spaced.

◀ **7**

Thread ribbon or cord through the holes, either to form two handles or to tie the bag closed.

letters COUNT!

by the Editor

We have ten numerals: 0, 1, 2, 3, 4, 5, 6, 7, 8, 9. When we want to describe a bigger number, we join two or more numerals together: 16, 235 or 999. If we want to have even bigger numbers, we still join up the numerals, but divide them up with commas, to make reading the number easier: 1,674, 5,555, 1,000,000. The only time we don't use a comma is when we are writing the date: 1992. But our way of writing numbers isn't the only one. Where might you see figures like this?

III XII IX V VII

It would probably help if you saw them as they actually appear:

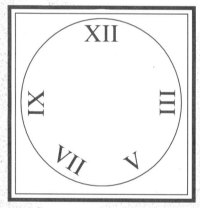

It's an old-fashioned clock face with what are called Roman numerals. The numerals we use today came to our country from the Orient hundreds of years ago, but before that we used these Roman numerals. The ancient Romans counted in tens, like we do, but they used ordinary letters from the alphabet to show numbers, and made up bigger numbers by joining the letters together.

I = 1
V = 5
X = 10

So they would write I for 1, II for 2, and III for 3. At first they used to write IIII for 4, and then V for 5, then VI (V + I) for 6, VII for 7 and VIII for 8. They would write bigger numbers by joining the letters together, like this:

XV = X + V = 10 + 5 = 15
XVIII = X + V + III = 10 + 5 + 3 = 18
X + X = 10 + 10 = 20
XXV = X + X + V = 10 + 10 + 5 = 25

After a while, everyone found some numbers were getting much too long to write out, so they decided to write IV for 4 and IX for 9.

IV = 1-before-5 (I-before-V)
IX = 1-before-10 (I-before-X)

And the same happened with bigger numbers:

XIV = 10 + 1-before-5 = 14
XIX = 10 + 1-before-10 = 19
XXIV = 10 + 10 + 1-before-five = 24

They also gave bigger numbers their own letters:

L = 50
C = 100
D = 500
M = 1,000

That meant that they could write down quite large numbers without taking up too much space. Instead of writing the number 90 like this:

XXXXXXXXX

they could write:

XC (10-before-100)

And if they had wanted to write out the year 1993, they could write out:

MCMXCIII

rather than:

MCCCCCCCCCCXXXXXXXXXIII

(Still not as easy as 1993, is it?)
We still sometimes use Roman numerals today – on stones giving the date when a building was opened, for instance, or in books to show the chapter numbers, or on sundials. If you look carefully at the end of a television programme you'll see the year the programme was made written in tiny Roman numerals.

So keep a Wide Awake eye open and see how many places you can spot Roman numerals still in use today!

WORDSQUARE

The names of five Sixes are hidden in this wordsquare – can you find them?

R	O	Y	G	B	Y	K
P	I	X	I	E	S	E
V	A	J	L	Q	P	L
L	L	V	W	O	R	P
N	E	G	A	C	I	I
S	W	E	L	T	T	E
L	G	N	O	M	E	S
D	P	W	N	P	S	J

WHERE ARE WE?

Some of the Six names are particularly associated with parts of the United Kingdom. Can you draw a line from each emblem to the part of the country you think he comes from? Of course, each one is found all over the UK now, not just in one place!

TAKE A PENCIL...

It's easy to draw your Six emblem!

First draw a circle for his head:

Then draw in the body:

Next look carefully at the arms, and draw them in place:

Do the same for the legs:

Add the details of his hat, or anything he is holding:

Then colour in and add eyes, nose and mouth:

Decorate your Six equipment with tiny dancing Elves, Kelpies, or whatever your Six is. They don't all have to be in the same position!

Answers to the puzzles on page 61.

FIRE! FIRE!

by the Editor
illustrated by Jane Hibbert

When you're a Guide you'll go to camp and get to know how to build and cook on a fire. You'll sit round it at night wrapped in a blanket and maybe you'll sing camp fire songs. The fire will be your friend – if you treat it very carefully. But a fire out of control is a very different thing from the friendly camp fire. Would you know what to do if you thought there was a fire at home?

If you have the Safety in the Home badge you'll know the things you need to do to help prevent a fire in your home:

- Turn off non-essential electrical gadgets (like televisions, lamps, computers, radios, etc) at the socket and pull the plugs out.
- Don't hang tea-towels over cookers.
- Don't fill chip pans more than half full.
- Close doors behind you when you go out.
- Don't play near open fires.
- Don't leave matches lying about.
- Make sure all cigarettes are properly out in ashtrays (or, better still, no one should smoke in the house at all!).
- Ask your parents to fit smoke alarms.

But if a fire happens in a room where you are, what should you do?

- Keep low – heat and smoke rise to the ceiling.
- Get everyone out of the room. Close the windows if it is safe. When everyone is out of the room, close the door behind you. Leave the house, closing the front door.
- Tell your neighbours and call the fire brigade – ring 999 from a public 'phone box or a neighbour's telephone.
- Don't go back into the house – wait in a safe place until the fire brigade arrives.

If you wake up and smell smoke or hear a fire:

- Roll out of bed on to the floor – remember to keep low.
- Crawl over to the door and feel with the back of your hand. If it is hot, don't open the door – shout to warn the other people in the house.
- Put your bedding at the bottom of the door, to fill any gap between the door and the floor and stop smoke coming through.
- Crawl to the window and open it. (If you have double glazing make sure the key is always near the window on a hook.) If it won't open, break it with a chair.
- Shout to neighbours or passers-by to call the fire brigade and wait at the window for the fire engine to arrive.

If the door is cold, carefully open it and look and look for smoke. If you can't see smoke, wake up everyone else and leave the house, closing windows and doors behind you, and ring the fire brigade as above.

HOW DOES FIRE BURN?

To make a fire, there must be a 'triangle':

HEAT – which can come from a match, or wires overheating, or a cooker flame. OXYGEN – which is usually all around in the air! FUEL – whatever is around and will burn.

Take away any one of these and the fire should go out, although sometimes just taking heat away isn't enough because the fire has enough heat of its own to keep going. That's why you have to cover a burning chip pan with a lid or damp tea-towel to put out the fire – turning the heat off helps but you have to take away the fire's oxygen supply by covering it.

Fire extinguishers work by taking away one or more of the parts of the triangle – usually heat or oxygen.

FIRE EXTINGUISHERS

You've probably noticed fire extinguishers at school, at the place where your Pack meets, in shops and other public places. Some people even have them at home in the kitchen or in their cars. Have you noticed that they are different colours?

The colour of the fire extinguisher usually (but not always) shows what's inside it. That's because although you can use water to put out lots of fires (your camp fire, for instance), it's not the right thing to use to put out some kinds of fire.

RED contains water and can be used on paper, wood or cloth fires. It should never be used on a fire where there is electricity (eg an overheating plug) or burning oil or fat.

BLACK contains carbon dioxide, which is a gas which stops things burning without getting them wet, so it's a good one to use on any fire, especially electrical or oil fires.

CREAM contains foam. It's good for oil fires because it smothers the flame, stopping oxygen getting to it, but it also contains water so it can't be used on electrical fires.

BLUE contains a dry powder which smothers the fire. It can be used on any kind of fire.

GREEN contains a gas – halon – which affects the flames so that they can't burn any more. It doesn't make a mess and is very good for computer or electrical fires.

Look round your school and Brownie meeting place and see what kinds of fire extinguisher there are. Are they the right ones for the job?

Here's how to make an extinguisher which will put out the flame on a candle.

You will need:

Bicarbonate of soda
Vinegar
A small jug with a thin pouring 'lip'
A jam jar with a lid
2 bendy straws
A candle and holder
Liquid soap for a foamy extinguisher

- Make two holes in the jam jar lid and carefully push the straws through them.
- Mix a tablespoonful of bicarbonate of soda powder with the liquid soap in the jam jar and put on the lid.
- Put the candle in its holder and light it. Aim one of the straws at the flame (not too close!)
- Carefully pour some vinegar down the other straw.

What happens? Experiment with different amounts of vinegar and bicarbonate of soda to find out which is the best combination.

MORE *Healthy* FUN

by Gillian Ellis   illustrated by Helen Herbert

Start healthy habits while you're young and they should last for life.

- Walk tall; don't slouch. Imagine you're carrying a heavy load on your head, as many girls do in Africa, and push up against it. Keep your head up, your bottom and tummy in, and your shoulders back. If you're extra tall, be proud of it! Don't try to hide the fact by slouching! Do remember that tall people are attractive if they walk beautifully – it's only when they try to hide their height that they become round-shouldered and spoil their figures.

- Take regular exercise, every day if you can. Most Brownies don't need too much encouragement to enjoy skipping ropes and ball games, even if they're alone!

- Make yourself a Healthy Eating Plan and talk about it with your mum or whoever buys the food in your home. Try to eat some of these foods every day: fresh vegetables and fruit; wholemeal bread or pasta; cheese, milk, yogurt or fromage frais, and, if your family eats meat, some chicken or white fish.

- Today's healthy Brownies are tomorrow's healthy mums!

Make up your mind now that you will never smoke cigarettes or try any drugs except those which a doctor prescribes to make you better when you're ill. All other drugs make you feel really horrible and smoking can damage your health in many ways.

- Look after your body, and it will look after you!

Here are some simple ways of keeping healthy. Try to do at least one of them every day, with a friend or alone.

Outdoors

- **Skipping** Set yourself challenges – try to reach 20, 50, 100 skipping forwards or backwards, or learn new fancy steps or to skip on alternate feet or on one foot only.

- **Ball skills** Just bounce a ball, or throw and catch with a friend. Play against a wall, with one, two or three balls and vary your game by bouncing the ball under your leg, or turning or clapping between catches.

- **Hoop skills** There is nothing like a session with a hula-hoop for keeping you trim!

- **Handstands** against a wall.

- **Balancing** on low narrow walls or upturned sturdy flowerpots.

- A brisk **walk**, even just round your garden.

- **Hopscotch** or leapfrog with a friend.

- **Throwing** balls or beanbags into a box. As you become good at this, move further away from the box.

58

Indoors on a wet day

- Walk round the room balancing a book on your head.
- Walk round balancing a ball on a book, held in the hand you don't write with.
- Make room to practise forward and backward rolls.
- **Stretching exercises** Feet together, touch your toes without bending knees; feet apart, touch right foot with left hand and vice versa. Lie flat and point toes towards ceiling. Ask someone to show you how to do press-ups.

A HEALTHY BODY ACROSTIC

Cover this when you sneeze

You need plenty of good fresh

Food passes from the stomach to this

When we breathe in, the air goes into our

We think with this

Our eyes need good light to help us do this

The kidneys produce this waste matter

Our food is digested here

This pumps blood round our bodies

When you have all the answers, the initial letters will form the name of something every healthy Brownie should own.

FITNESS FOODS FOR BRIGHT BROWNIES

See if you can unscramble the letters below to find some foods to keep you healthy!

KLIM   RROCTA REBCCMUU   PLAPE   NNAABA BAGCEBA
SHEEEC DREAB   TAPOOT   ARNEGO   ARPE   ULTECTE
ARDSHI SNEAB   FLICAUWRELO APES   PRAGES RRECISEH

Answers on page 61.

MISSING LETTERS

Fit in the missing letters to find ten activities which will help to keep you fit.

T- -LE - -NN-S; R-NN- -G;
-WI- - -NG; HO- - - R- - -NG;
NE- -AL-; -KA-I- -; WA- -I-G;
- -N-IS; - -CK-Y; -Y-N-S-I-S.

A SKIP
TO BEAT
BAD
temper

by Cynthia Mitchell
illustrated by Jan Lewis

An angry tiger in a cage
Will roar and roar with rage,
And gnash his teeth and lash his tail,
For that's how tigers rant and rail.
I keep my temper in a cage,
I hate it when it roars with rage,
I hate its teeth, I hate its tail,
So when it starts to rant and rail,
I tell my mum, I tell my dad,
I tell them why it's feeling bad,
And then I skip and skip and skip,
And lash my rope just like a whip
And when I skip because I'm cross,
My temper-tiger knows who's boss,
And when I've skipped and whipped like mad,
My temper-tiger's not so bad.
I have to keep it tame this way,
Or it will eat me up one day.

From *Halloweena Hecate* published by
William Heinemann Ltd.

Every effort has been made to reach the copyright holder of this
poem. The Girl Guides Association would be glad to hear from
anyone whose rights they have unknowingly infringed.

Puzzle time on page 7

Jumbled up Sixes: Imps, Kelpies, Elves, Sprites, Gnomes, Pixies.

What's missing?: The head of the Gnome's broom, the plume from the Kelpie's hat, a leg of the Bwbachod's stool, one of the Imp's ears, the top of the Leprechaun's hat, the Elf's smile.

Lend a hand crossword on page 13

Across: 4. Shine; 6. Polish; 7. Good Turn; 9. Important; 10. Yuk.

Down: 1. Washing up; 2. Neighbourly; 3. Clean; 5. You; 8. Thank.

How's your general knowledge? on page 27

Books and stories: 1. Cinderella; 2. Roald Dahl; 3. The dark; 4. Jack; 5. Narnia.

The world: 1. The English Channel; 2. India; 3. Island; 4. Japan; 5. Holland (Netherlands).

Animals, birds and trees: 1. Gosling; 2. Six; 3. Butterfly; 4. Cuckoo; 5. Lion.

Your body: 1. Pupil; 2. Ten – it's another name for your fingers and thumbs; 3. Two; 4. Your baby teeth (the ones that grow first and then drop out); 5. Your throat (larynx).

Anything goes: 1. Gold, silver and bronze, in that order; 2. Kaleidoscope; 3. Minnie; 4. William Shakespeare; 5. Shuttlecock.

Pirate puzzles on page 31

Letter: Dear Daisy, The postman will bring a parcel each day. We hope you enjoy being a pirate too. Please get well soon, Love and kisses, the Brownies.

Thursday's secret message: Pirate party at 2pm. Make Pieces of Eight. Box and recipe in shed.

More puzzles on page 55

Wordsquare:

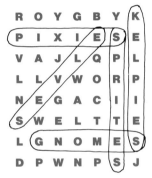

Where are we? Leprechaun – Ulster; Gillie Dhu and Kelpies – Scotland; Pixies – Cornwall; Bwbachod – Wales.

More healthy fun! on page 59

A healthy body acrostic: Nose; Air; Intestine; Lungs; Brain; Read; Urine; Stomach; Heart. Hidden word: NAILBRUSH.

Fitness foods: Milk; Carrot; Cucumber; Apple; Banana; Cabbage; Cheese; Bread; Potato; Orange; Pear; Lettuce; Radish; Beans; Cauliflower; Peas; Grapes; Cherries.

Missing letters: Table tennis; Running; Swimming; Horse riding; Netball; Skating; Walking; Tennis; Hockey; Gymnastics.

pac-a-sac!

by Heather Welford   illustrated by Helen Herbert

The Elves are getting ready for Pack Holiday! Who can get their rucsac ready first? Play the game overleaf and find out!

How to play

Any number between two and six can play. Decide on your names first, and give each person a button or a counter to move up and down the board. You'll also need a dice, plus a piece of paper and a pencil. Write down each player's name, followed by 's' for socks, 'b' for boots, 'u' for underwear, 'j' for jumper and 'c' for coat.

You can only pack the items you need in your rucsac when you land on the right square. You need a six to come on to the first square (with the rucsac on it) but once on the board, you can collect your items in any order you like.

In this game, you can move your counter up or down your line of squares, but in one direction only per turn. So, if you throw a three, you can move your counter up three squares or down three squares. When you land on a piece of clothing you can 'pack' it, by ticking it off the list next to your name.

You must move somewhere, even if you throw a six and you are in the middle of the board, which would take you to the finish point (you aren't actually finished until you've packed everything, so you'll have to move downwards again after your next turn).

When you have collected all your items, you can head for the bus – but you can only finish by throwing the exact number to land on the finish point.

The winner is the first person to get to the finish, fully packed. Happy holidays!

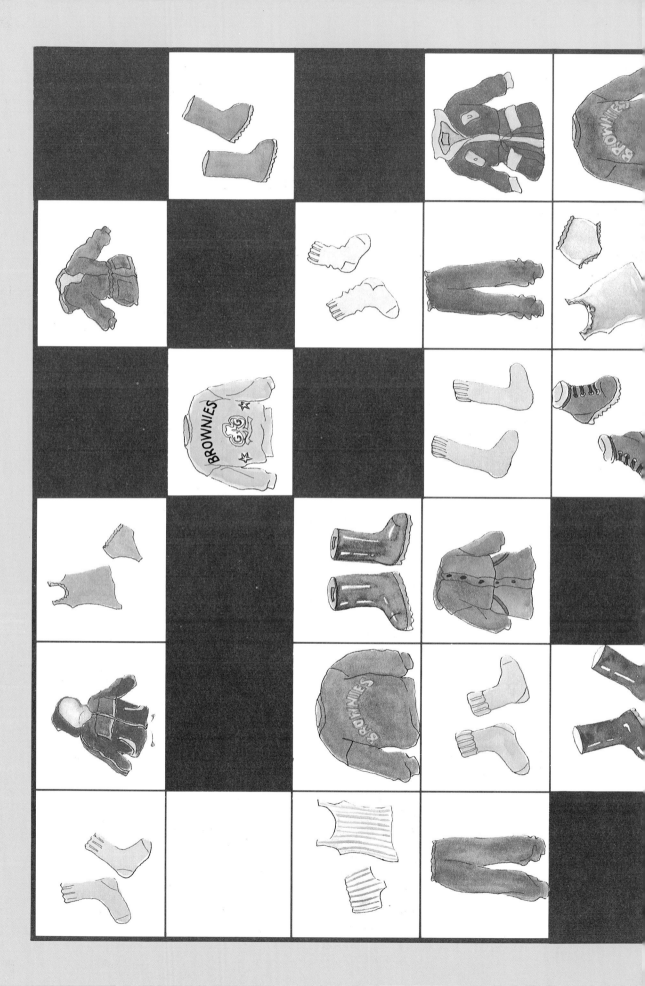